A TREE HAS ROOTS

Harry Smith

Faithbuilders Publishing
49 Kingmere, South Terrace
Littlehampton, BN17 5LD, United Kingdom
www.faithbuilderspublishing.co.uk

ISBN: 978-1-913181-94-9

First edition: September 2023.

Edited by Harry Smith
Cover art by Nigel Smith (hello@wolfandbear.co)
Layout by David Powell
Printed in the United Kindgom

Contents

3

Endorsements

Rev Dr Ken Newell
Minister Emeritus, Fitzroy Presbyterian Church,
Belfast, Northern Ireland
Pax Christi International Peace Prize Recipient (1999)
Moderator of the Presbyterian Church in Ireland (2004-2005)

During the long, dark night of Northern Ireland's Troubles (1968 -1998) I was agonised with questions: 'How can we end the carnage? Can hardened political attitudes ever give way to a vision for partnership? Why are churches, cocooned in spiritual apartheid, so resistant to becoming centres of peacemaking?

With acute historical precision, A Tree Has Roots exposes some major blocking mechanisms to reconciliation within the Ulster psyche: the Doctrine of Discovery and the Empire spirit that always seeks to dominate. We are urged to abandon 'the futile ways inherited from our ancestors' (1 Peter) and embrace Christ's message of bonding across all our divisions.

The Right Rev Harold Millar,
Former Church of Ireland Bishop,
Down and Dromore Diocese (1997-2019)

Harry Smith has lived out a God-given calling, over the past couple of decades, to remind the Church, and especially the historic churches in Ireland, of our less-than-comfortable history. In this, his most recent book, A Tree has Roots, he takes us on a very informative journey through the history of the church since the time of Constantine, when Church and State became unhelpfully intertwined. He enables us to see some of the spiritual damage that has resulted, especially in the not-well-known and very damaging Doctrine of Discovery.

A Tree has Roots is calling not just individuals, but church institutions, to recognition and repentance. This is worked out in the context of indigenous people in North America, but more specifically in the context of Ireland, where so many of the issues of religious power, pride and division have been focussed. The question is 'Do we see the issues, and the present effects of them?', and then the deeper question 'What do we do now to find freedom, so that we don't carry them into another generation?' This book opens up the questions in a challenging and informative way.

Fr. Martin Magill
Parish Priest, St John the Evangelist, Belfast

In this booklet Harry Smith shares his personal journey which has led him to speak into our pain filled and broken society. He has chosen a particularly challenging topic in the form of the Covenant issue. From my own personal perspective Harry's thinking and this writing has helped me in my understanding of what has shaped our past in Northern Ireland/Ireland and continues to play a role in how our future is unfolding. I happen to believe this booklet has an important part to play in a deeper understanding of some of the issues affecting our global community at this time.

As a church leader, I was challenged to reflect on the way clergy and people of faith have used scripture to justify their own positions. Harry raises serious issues which need to be considered by the faith community throughout Ireland and beyond around what has been done "in the name of God". I endorse Harry's words: "I would love to see small groups of Clergy and/or members of their congregation informally getting together, to re-examine our history and its legacy. Not with any sectarian, political agendas but solely for 'the Kingdom of God and His righteousness'. To seek His face, embrace His heart!" As I look at our deeply divided society I value this publication and I add my support to Harry's words: "The prophetic role of the Church is to repent for what we have wrongly done in the land and give a courageous lead. God is calling us to the ministry of reconciliation, to be His healers in the land".

David Legge,
Bible Teacher and author

A Tree Has Roots is a fascinating and insightful read into some lesser-known facts concerning our shared national and religious histories. Before we can 'move on,' we often have to look back and dig deep to uncover the hidden things of darkness that hinder us. I would encourage Christians (especially church leaders) to read this book and prayerfully and humbly consider some of the sins of church and empire that may have bound us in measure even to this day. Harry Smith, as always, has done a fantastic job of research, and I pray his latest offering will have a significant impact, especially in our native Ireland.

Andy Smith, Senior Pastor
Belfast City Vineyard

As ever, Harry Smith reminds us that our individual and collective choices and allegiances have profound spiritual consequences. In his writing and analysis, he never fails to courageously call the church to the tasks of repentance, forgiveness, and peacemaking. He has lived a life of intercession and courageous obedience to Jesus which comes through clearly as he invites readers to consider how we can give our allegiance to Jesus alone and be builders of His kingdom in these lands.

Margaret Clarke
Director, Transformations-Ireland

I have known Harry for a long time and have journeyed with him as he has diligently researched and listened to God over many years on the issues raised in this booklet. He writes in a very personal style, yet all of the major points raised are well researched and referenced. I urge you to prayerfully read this account and begin to recognise some of the things he feels have held us back, and impeded unity and working together both in church and society. If properly addressed at a deep and personal level, these matters have the potential to very profoundly alter our ability to walk in true unity and to see true progress against some of the big blockages we have in society.

Rev. Peter Murray
Former President, Methodist Church in Ireland (2014-15)

Many sincere folk have never heard of the Doctrine of Discovery. This booklet shows how it fostered an era of colonising exploitation that continues to contaminate every aspect of life for millions of people across the world. Harry Smith makes a strong case for the church to face up to its part in empire expansion which was legitimised by this false doctrine. He pleads for a spirit of humility and repentance that *will release blessing on the earth. I hope and pray that we are up to the challenge of this prophetic call.*

Fergus McMorrow
Director of Divine Healing Ministries
N. Ireland

The significance and importance of this book by Harry Smith cannot be overstated. This is more than a book; this is a prophetic urging that shines a light into strongholds across the Church and society, strongholds that the Lord is waiting for His people to recognise and to bring down in repentance. A Tree has Roots not only shines a light into the deep roots and the implications of the "Doctrine of Discovery", but it presents ways the Lord offers for healing, particularly to see a movement of prayer rising up, to come against the "principalities and powers" operating in this land.

I have found that reading and praying through this book has helped to "connect the dots" regarding the historical and spiritual issues that continue to impact this generation. This is a book that provokes a response, impacting how we pray for the land and how we live and witness as the Church, the nation's only hope.

Foreword

I want to take this opportunity to introduce myself and also thank you for reading this booklet.

I grew up in Belfast, where I spent the first thirty years of my life. After completing my Secondary Education, I enrolled on a new course at the Royal Victoria Hospital, Belfast, that combined General and Psychiatric Nurse training. On qualifying, I went on to do further training in Intensive Care Nursing and also became a Clinical Nurse Educator. This all took place with the background of civil unrest in Northern Ireland - known as "the troubles." It was also during this period that I had an encounter with God as the Charismatic Renewal began, which led to a deeper understanding of intercession and of God's heart for reconciliation.

In 1979 my wife Dorothy and I left nursing to participate in a Training Course in the Netherlands for the ministry of Healthcare Christian Fellowship International - which majored in providing discipleship and evangelistic training among health field personnel. Over the following thirteen years I first of all headed up the work here in Ireland, based in Dublin, before taking on the role of Prayer Coordinator of the work in the Europe Headquarters, based in the Netherlands. This took me to most of the countries in Europe working with the National Staff and enabled me to have the privilege of networking with many of Europe's Prayer and Reconciliation ministries.

In 1992 we returned to Northern Ireland, to join the residential community at the Christian Renewal Centre, in Rostrevor, Co. Down, where I became the Prayer Coordinator. I also served on the leadership team alongside the Rev. Cecil and Myrtle Kerr, its founders. When they retired in 2000, we took up the helm for the ensuing ten years. Early in my time there, God highlighted to me a major issue concerning the Ulster Covenant of 1912, which led to the writing of the book: *Heal not Lightly*.

We left the Centre in 2010, returning to Belfast to enjoy a much-needed break before I embarked on the next phase of my journey: writing, research and involving myself in ministry with others in North America related to Native/White American reconciliation issues. During this research I discovered that a seed of division was sown here, as far back as 1155, when the Roman Catholic King, Henry II, was given full papal authority to subdue Ireland. Out of that seed a substantial tree has grown which has traversed the Reformation - it has many branches. One of these, is related to the Ulster Covenant which started my journey. With these insights, I am now back full circle to look at and explore the deeply rooted historic divisions in Ireland.

Part I

Introduction - my journey

Back in September 2019, I had the privilege of joining with over one thousand people in St. Anne's Cathedral, Belfast, for the 'Soul of the Nation' prayer gathering. It was related to a decision made by the British Parliament, in the absence of a functioning Northern Ireland Assembly, to force through legislation – counter to existing laws here - on abortion. It is incredible how a critical issue like that, can unite us in prayer unto God.

I came away from it wondering what it would be like to have similar gatherings happening all over this island, calling upon God to see our idols of nationalism (Irish and Protestant/Unionist - expressed through covenants) being laid down and especially the latter, being repented of by the governing bodies of the Presbyterian, Church of Ireland and Methodist Churches in Ireland?

What will it take for us, as the family of God, of all traditions, to grasp the significance of that, in the same way, as we did over the abortion issue in the Cathedral that evening? We came together because we understood the gravity of the situation. Sadly, we are nowhere near there, when it comes to issues like the Ulster Covenant of 1912 and the Sinn Fein Covenant of 1916 and the history surrounding them, in our land!

For me, this has been a key issue for many years and one that I want to explore with you in this booklet. And yet, these two covenants are only a small part of our divided history in Ireland and need to be put into a much wider context, understood, and owned. My concern is that we do not know our own cultures history, never mind that of the other. If we did, we would be on our knees before God in repentance for the way we have embraced the negative legacies passed down to us. This was highlighted in May 2020, following the death of George Floyd in

11

the US, after which so many Americans expressed that they did not know their own history. Following that, both here in the UK and the US, many people have been revisiting their nations' respective histories and asking searching questions. Questions regarding the colonial-era statues erected to celebrate what had been done in the name of Empire expansion regarding black slavery and the Native American Nations. There have also been a number of historical documentaries here in the UK that have been highlighting aspects of the negative legacies of the British Empire era – many large stately homes were built out of the profits from the sugar and cotton plantations of the Caribbean!

The subject of Covenants in Ireland is one that I have carried in prayer, research, and writing for nearly thirty years. As I have already mentioned, after leaving the Christian Renewal Centre, I had a break of approximately eight years from this as a specific focus, as I knew that God had asked me to lay it down to concentrate on another research issue: the role Great Britain and Ireland played in establishing the original thirteen American Colonies. Interestingly, this focus on America's roots only served to give me greater insight and clarity regarding the Covenants in Ireland. I am now in a new season focusing again on Ireland's roots, and indeed, if anything, my interest in and the burden of prayer regarding these Covenants have significantly intensified over the past four years, since returning to the subject.

The Covenant issue has been a huge one to embrace and most certainly not one that I have wanted to pick up again on my own. Regarding that, in 2019 I met with a few folks who have walked the journey with me, some of them, over many years. During one of our prayer times, someone shared a picture God gave them: it was of a 'line out' in a game of rugby. As the ball was thrown in, the other team members (the forwards) lifted up one of their members, to retrieve the ball. When that person caught it, it was brought to ground and the team gathered protectively around him/the ball – the intent being either to push forward hoping to score or to pass it out to the other team members (the backs). The understanding we received from that was that I was the one being lifted up, and the ball was the issue of the Ulster Covenant and its greater historic context. The reassuring thing for me was, that I was not alone, that there would also be others out there, with a similar heart, working together!

This journey in research, discussion, and prayer, has resulted in the publication of two books. The first one is called *Heal Not Lightly*[1] and the second one – *A Destiny Denied... A Dignity Restored.*[2]

Heal Not Lightly

This book is about issues that led to the partitioning of Ireland in 1921 and the birth of Northern Ireland and the Republic of Ireland: The Ulster Covenant (1912); the Easter Proclamation (1916) and the Civil War. The reality is, that both groups are, as a result of these covenants, profoundly opposed to each other. Yet, both are expressions of nationalism! The book also speaks of the key leadership role the major Protestant Churches played in the drawing up and signing of the Ulster Covenant, with the ongoing repercussions for the whole island.

The journey I have been on regarding the spiritual legacy of the past on current events in Ireland all started with a dream I had in 1993:

> "It was a very vivid, full-colour movie picture of a beaver's dam. To the left of it, the ground was dry and barren, with only a few trickles of water filtering through. Along their courses there was vegetation. On the right of the dam, a large volume of water was being retained. I could see people on the dam itself, working in an attempt to dismantle it. They knew that the water needed to be released so that it could flow across the barren ground. Yet, they were equally aware that they were not being very successful!
>
> I was then taken down under the water, which was being held back by the dam, to its foundations. There I saw a large log positioned across the full length of it, with the words "The Ulster Covenant" written on it. I then heard a voice speaking to me, "If you want to see this water flow out across the land, then you must remove the log in the foundations of this dam." The "you" mentioned here had a very personal implication and also a wider corporate dimension to it." (From the Introduction of *"Heal Not Lightly."*)

I instinctively knew that the water represented the Holy Spirit. I also knew what God was pointing at: that the Protestant Church in this land had put that log in place. In doing so, it had grieved and quenched the Holy Spirit! Alongside that, it became clear to me in my research that we had used our hatred and fear of the Catholic Church, alongside the drawing up of a covenant (emulating the precedent set in Scotland in 1638) as a tool to unite the Protestant community against the British Government's Home Rule Bill.

Having been involved over many years, with others in the UK and Europe, in reconciliation and prayer ministries, I have learned that national level intercession must go hand in hand with in-depth research. After such an encounter with God, I knew I had to hit the research trail – hard! That research journey took me back into 1912; the Home Rule Bill; the Plantation of Ulster and the Scottish Covenanters.

In the book *Heal Not Lightly*, I also wrote about another significant dream I had had in 1998. It was about two magnets. In it, I saw two groups of people trying to bring together the positive poles of two large magnets, which, as I expected, repelled each other. I knew that the two people groups were the British and Irish Governments who were seeking to bring together the two magnets, representing the Democratic Unionist Party (DUP) and Sinn Féin. Like the magnets they could only repel each other – both, after all, were seeking totally opposite outcomes from the political process and both had their political ideologies concretised in covenants. These two parties are best described as being in a counter-covenantal relationship! I had a strong sense that, built into this political process, was the capacity for it to collapse.

I had this dream not long after the signing of the Good Friday Agreement (also known as the Belfast Agreement) which was the culmination of a long-drawn-out peace process. It led, the following year, to the formation of the Power-Sharing Executive. As the logic of the magnet image suggests, the Executive and the Assembly has already experienced dissolution: in fact, four times - two short periods in 2002, 2011, a longer one, from 2017 to January 2020. The current one – at the time of writing - is connected to Brexit, the Protocol, and the Assembly Election in May 2022. This is a fragile union; clearly, as Jesus said in Matthew 12:25, *"Every kingdom... divided against itself will not stand."*

Unfortunately, many are looking for a political answer to what is primarily a spiritual issue.

In *"The Spirit of the Disciplines: Understanding how God changes lives,"*[3] Dallas Willard wrote:

> "The World can no longer be left to mere diplomats, politicians and business leaders. They have done the best they could, no doubt. But this is an age for spiritual heroes – a time for men and women to be heroic in faith and in spiritual character and power. The greatest danger to the Christian church today is that of pitching its message too low."

What I want to see is the Irish Church leadership stepping up to the plate regarding this issue. All too often in the past, when there has been a serious paramilitary incident and someone is murdered, local clergy make a joint statement, appealing to the political system to address it. Important as that is, I feel that they are "pitching the message too low." One possible reason for this is that they do not appear to make a connection with what is going on in the heavenly realms. This is what we as Christians are meant to do! We are engaged in something that the Apostle Paul describes as a battle that "*is not against flesh and blood but against the rulers, against the powers of this dark world and against the spiritual forces of evil in the heavenly realms.*" Ephesians 6:12. Once I began to read history through this lens, something changed in my spirit. I began to see things from a different perspective.

John Dawson, Founder of the International Reconciliation Coalition, in his book *"Taking your Cities for God"* puts it this way:

> "The only authority Satan has is a stolen human authority. He initially gains this authority when, at some point in history, human beings believe his lie, receive his accusation and are seduced into an allegiance to his plan... Whole countries are kept in darkness by satanic lies that have become cornerstones of a particular culture."[4]

In *"What Christians Should Know About Reconciliation,"* he also writes:

> "Our primary objective in intercession and spiritual warfare is not the removal of the enemy but the return of the glory – the restoration of God's needed favour, reconciliation with God. When we encounter a spiritual stronghold, it is not a testimony to the presence of a big demon, but rather to the absence of the glory. Just as nature abhors a vacuum, so it is in the unseen realm. When the glory departs, the demons rush in. We have an enemy that swarms to open wounds and corruption – a characteristic revealed in the name, Beelzebub (Luke 11:15), which means 'lord of the flies.' His weapons are accusation and deception, his strongholds are places of unresolved guilt and unhealed wounds within the land."

> "A repentant church, confessing the sins of the nation before God is that nation's only hope… The unredeemed cannot make atonement for the land. The pagan cannot go up into the gap and present the blood of the Lamb… Our nation will be cursed, or blessed, according to the obedience or disobedience of the Church."[5]

In general, I have found that our theology regarding the 'spirit realms' has been poor – we just don't see it. Yet, in 2 Corinthians 10:3-5 we read about strongholds, arguments and pretensions; in Ephesians 4:26-27 Paul alerts us to the danger of giving the devil a foothold: *"In your anger do not sin! Do not let the sun go down while you are still angry, and do not give the devil a foothold."* The broad principle in this is - sin that is not repented of, gives Satan a foothold in our lives. Whether in a marriage, a church or a nation, Satan is, thereby, given a legal right to operate. That becomes all the more noteworthy when we make covenants against each other. On the island of Ireland, the counter-covenantal dynamic in our relationships has given Satan an open opportunity to operate in the political and spiritual life of each respective nation here.

We teach about putting the whole armour on, but what for? The scriptures mentioned above need to be unpacked and earthed into our everyday lives. My experience has been that many Protestant clergy are under the influence of the spiritual stronghold of the Ulster Covenant which their forefathers signed and sadly they don't realise it. It's not that they won't see it, they can't see it. They are also, in many cases, locked into this pervasive stronghold within their denominations. To flow against the stream is not an easy call. To expose this history may risk them losing their pulpit ministry and dividing their congregations (their words, not mine). They most certainly need our prayers and support.

Over the three-year period of a non-functioning government (between January 2017 and January 2020), there had often been talks in terms of renewed hope, of getting the political process going again. However, the hope expressed has sounded more like the 'hope' of 'I hope so' rather than the type of hope Paul writes about in Romans 8:22-25:

> *"We know that the whole creation has been groaning as in the pains of childbirth right up to the present time. Not only so, but we ourselves, who have the first fruits of the Spirit, groan inwardly as we wait eagerly for our adoption to sonship, the redemption of our bodies. For in this hope we were saved. But hope that is seen is no hope at all. Who hopes for what they already have? But if we hope for what we do not yet have, we wait for it patiently."*

In that image of the beaver dam, mentioned above, was a huge reservoir of water being held back – the river of His Spirit. Throughout scripture that river flows from the temple (Ezekiel 47, Revelation 22). The Church is now collectively, that temple! In John 7:37-38, Jesus said that out of us would flow rivers of living water. Herein lies something of God's heart for the Church in Ireland.

I long for the day when repentance flows and that dam is breached; when a tsunami of the Spirit flows through this land, sweeping aside all that is not of Him! This is my deeply held hope – though I wait, sometimes not all that patiently, for its fulfilment!

***

When we left the Christian Renewal Centre my direction of ministry was changing to a focus on America and Native American issues. This meant, at the time, laying the Covenant issue here in Ireland, aside.

A Destiny Denied... A Dignity Restored

This book is primarily about North America: its British colonial foundations and the beginnings of an ongoing negative relationship with the Native American nations - before and after the War of Independence. It's about the expansion of Empire and the ongoing effects this had on the Native Nations. Nations like Spain, Portugal, France and England were the aggressors. Some people in Ireland have told me that this book has given them an even more in-depth understanding of the historic issues in Ireland's relationship with England, before and after the Reformation – even though that was not my primary reason for writing it!

In a real sense, this book was born out of the first one. It started with a question that I had carried unanswered since the early days of researching my first book – the issue of Oliver Cromwell. I wondered how he as a Puritan, evangelical, Bible-believing Christian, a radical product of the Reformation and vehemently anti-Catholic, could come to Ireland and so violently suppress its Irish Catholics and Royalist allies. Finding the answer to that was pivotal in writing this booklet.

I will pick up on Cromwell's genocidal actions in Ireland in Part II. At this point it is sufficient to mention that twelve years earlier, the Puritans in America, believing that God was on their side, murdered 700 men, women and children of the Pequot Tribe, in what became known as the Fort Mystic Massacre. Captain John Underhill wrote the following in his justification of the massacre of the Pequots:

> "... I would refer you to David's war. When a people is grown to such a height of blood, and sin against God and man... there he hath no respect to persons, but harrows them, and saws them, and puts them to the sword, and the most terriblest death that may be: sometimes the Scripture declareth women and children must perish with their parents; sometimes the case alters: but we will not dispute it now. We had sufficient light from the word of God for our proceedings..."[6]

Reading of this use of Scripture heightened my desire to get answers!

Part II
The Empire spirit!

In my quest for an answer I was sensing that God was saying to me – "Look back!" This brought my search back to the Reformation and then still further back into Catholic Church history.

The Doctrine of Discovery

When I came across a previously unknown term for me - the Doctrine of Discovery (DOD) - I knew in my spirit, that I was on to something. It is the term given to an ever-evolving process, over many centuries, originating from within the Vatican, and used to legally, politically and theologically justify empire expansion. I believe it is important to take you, the reader, back there, because when we talk about understanding the issue of roots in Ireland – we are looking at the early days in the development of the Doctrine of Discovery and the critical role it played in justifying Britain's expansion into here. Interestingly, in the United States, the DOD (now synonymous with the terms Manifest Destiny and White Exceptionalism) is very much to the fore regarding reconciliation issues regarding White, Native and Black Americans.

In the 1400s, prior to the Reformation, at the very start of European colonial expansion into the New World, Spain and Portugal made use of Papal bulls, underpinned by the Doctrine of Discovery, to justify colonising the Americas. According to Wikipedia, a papal bull "is a type of public decree, letters patent, or charter issued by a pope of the Catholic Church. It is named after the leaden seal (*bulla*) that was traditionally appended to the end in order to authenticate it."[7] This was understood and respected by two other major maritime nations at the time, England and France – who clearly understood what they were not mandated to

19

do. They could only trade, not colonise, knowing that excommunication awaited them if they attempted to establish their own colonies.

> "In a nutshell, the Doctrine of Discovery is one of the earliest examples of international law. It encapsulates a gradually developing and evolving process over many centuries, which became the accepted legal principle being applied by the Catholic Church to "Christian" European nations as they related to each other regarding the control of trade, exploration, and colonisation of non-European countries. It was also used to justify the domination of non-Christian peoples. Following the Reformation, England continued to use it, in its Protestantised form, in the North American colonies and further afield in Australia and New Zealand as the British Empire grew. With regards to Ireland, England's oldest colony, attempts at subjugating it had been going on for centuries without any direct mention of the term in the history books (though, as I have written earlier, back then the DOD was very much in the early stages of its development)!"[8]

As already mentioned, I discovered that the Catholic DOD was Protestantised after the Reformation, especially during the reign of Elizabeth I with the aid of Lord Chief Justice Coke. The "papal bull" was replaced by the issuing of Royal Charters. By the time of the American War of Independence, it was well established into the political, legal and theological thinking of what was to become the United States of America, to appear as the doctrine of Manifest Destiny in 1843.

***

To understand better the relevancy of the Doctrine of Discovery to the English and then British, colonisation of Ireland, we need to take a closer look at the origins and early evolution of the Doctrine in Europe.

A seed is sown

Every tree starts with a seed and I believe that the original seed for this tree was sown back in 313AD (Edict of Milan) when Emperor Constantine embraced Christianity. In 380AD, his successor, Theodosius, issued the Edict of Thessalonica, which not only forbade the practice of pagan religions but it also proclaimed Christianity to be the religion of the Empire. Unfortunately, what became known as Christendom was born: Christianity without any necessary conversion experience, intertwined with the politics of the Roman Empire, in what has been described as an 'empire spirit' - no longer solely an expression of the Kingdom of God. Needless to say, in the midst of this, there were also credible expressions of Christianity being lived out.

In 2 Corinthians 2:11, the Apostle Paul wrote: *"... we are not unaware of his [Satan's] schemes."* The birth of Christendom is one of his biggest schemes in history. Ripples from it have gone out ever since. We have been seduced by it many times!

The soil

I am using the image of 'soil' in two ways, yet both in the Bible are often inter-connected:

1.Metaphorical. This is the 'soil' of the human heart, composed of the fallen nature of mankind: pride, anger, bitterness, jealousy, division, murder, lies, power, control... It is a medium, a place in each of us, in which wrong actions/attitudes/thoughts can find a place to grow - often recognised in the scriptures as the heart of man.

2. A spiritual dynamic connected to real soil - literal. The first time this was recorded in the Bible is with regards to Cain murdering Abel, not long after Adam and Eve chose their way rather than God's. In Genesis 4:10 God addresses Cain: *"What have you done? Listen! Your brothers blood cries out to me from the ground."* Sin polluted the earth!

In Leviticus 18:24-25 we read, *"Do not defile yourselves in any of these ways (the context is regarding sexual sins), because this is why the nations that I am going to drive out before you became defiled. Even the land was defiled; so, I punished it for its sins, and the land vomited out its inhabitants."*

When God made a covenant with Abraham, He promised them the early and the latter rain which ensured a harvest. The absence of rain (drought) was a sign that they had sinned, broken covenant. We read about this in Deuteronomy 11:13-17 (RSV):

> *"And if you will obey my commandments which I command you this day, to love the Lord your God, and to serve him with all your heart and with all your soul, he will give the rain for your land in its season, the early rain and the later rain, that you may gather in your grain and your wine and your oil. And he will give grass in your fields for your cattle, and you shall eat and be full. Take heed lest your heart be deceived, and you turn aside and serve other gods and worship them, and the anger of the Lord be kindled against you, and he shut up the heavens, so that there be no rain, and the land yield no fruit, and you perish quickly off the good land which the Lord gives you."* (see also: Leviticus 26 & Deuteronomy 28.)

It's a scary thought, that sinful actions appear to pollute the physical earth. Ireland's soil which has been polluted with the blood of countless thousands who have died in genocidal actions or in revenge killing over centuries of warfare - often in the name of British Empire expansion - can continue to cry out for an acknowledgement, repentance, reconciliation, healing and justice.

The trunk (which grew out of the original seed planted in 313AD)

The papacy sought through its teaching on Petrine succession to affirm its authority/supremacy, even over the kings of Europe. This was to be developed over hundreds of years, to eventually manifest itself in one particular form, known as a "papal bull." But, let us start with Gregory VII (1073-85), who on ascending the papal throne made the declaration, that as the successor to St. Peter, he had been given universal rulership over Christendom. This included the secular rulers of his day: the kings and emperors.

Moving forward to 1302, Pope Boniface VIII was to add an important contribution to the debate. In the conclusion of his *Unam Sanctum*, we read: "[it] is altogether necessary to salvation for every human creature to be subject to the Roman pontiff." As Robert Williams puts it in his book, *"The American Indian in Western Legal Thought: The Discourse of Conquest."*

> "Only by the pope's implementation of a Christian government on a world scale, using Christian princes and armies, would the ecclesiastical society... be realized. That of course, was the idea of the Crusades, grounded in the universal Church's assertion of a divine right to enforce its vision of truth in all lands and cultures, Christian and non-Christian alike."[9]

In the midst of this, the Doctrine of Discovery was being consolidated. Through it, Satan was being given the freedom to operate within many countries around the world, negatively affecting their churches, politics and their relationships with each other and sadly, among the indigenous nations in their midst.

Over 800 years after Constantine, that tree was to produce another main branch here in Ireland (1155), by the English King – Henry II and Pope Adrian IV - with yet a further one forming with the arrival of the Reformation.

Westward bound

By the mid-1400s, both Portugal and Spain had been developing the means to make long-distance sea travel possible, and a clash of interests soon became inevitable when the Canary Islands were "discovered" by Portugal in the mid-Atlantic. With the initial motive of 'protecting' the islanders - converts, and infidels - the Church intervened, with Pope Eugenius IV issuing a papal bull in 1434 (*Creator Omnium*), which banned all Europeans from further involvement there. This decision, however, was contested by King Duarte of Portugal in 1436, arguing that their explorations were conquests, done on behalf of Christianity and that the Church now had a role to play, of being a guardian to the infidels.

Robert Miller in *"Native America Discovered and Conquered,"* puts it like this:

> "The conversion of the infidel natives was justified... because they allegedly did not have a common religion or laws; lacked normal social intercourse, money, metal, writing, and European-style clothing and lived like animals. The king claimed that the Canary converts to Christianity had made themselves subjects of Portugal and had now received the benefits of civil laws and organized society. Moreover, the King argued that the pope's ban interfered with this advance of civilization and Christianity that the king had commenced out of the goodness of his heart, 'more indeed for the salvation of the souls of the pagans of the islands than for his own personal gain.'"[10]

The pope then performed an about-turn which led to a significant revision of the DOD. When his legal advisors recalled the deliberations of Pope Innocent IV in 1240, Eugenius confirmed under what is known as the Law of Nations, that while the Canary Islanders had a right to dominium (governmental sovereignty and property), the papacy would keep a supervisory control over their secular activities. He would only step in if he thought that they violated European defined Natural Law [See footnote] or didn't want to have Christian missionaries among them. That was concretised by the pope issuing another bull in 1436 - *Romanus Pontifex* - which gave Portugal the authority to not only convert the people of the Canary Islands but also to oversee the islands on his behalf.

In 1452 the bull - *Dum Diversas* - was issued by Pope Nicholas V. It was decidedly aggressive, giving Portugal authority "to invade, search out, capture, vanquish, and subdue all Saracens and pagans" and to place them into perpetual slavery and to take all their property. A further rendition of *Romanus Pontifex* was made by him in 1455, enabling Portugal to expand its empire along the west coast of Africa. These papal bulls

Footnote: This is a concept of international law within the ancient Roman legal system and the Western Law traditions which are either based on or influenced by it. It is not a body of statute law or legal code, but rather customary law which is thought to be held in common by all people and nations in reasoned compliance with standards of international conduct.

demonstrated the developing meaning of the DOD at that time. They recognised the pope's interest to bring all humankind to the one true religion; authorised Portugal's work towards Christian conversion and civilisation and recognised Portugal's title and sovereignty over lands "which had already been acquired and which shall be in the future." and to accumulate enormous wealth through the extractions of precious minerals. It also led to the development of the black African slave trade.

How was Portugal's neighbour - a recently united Kingdom of Spain under King Ferdinand of Aragon and Queen Isabella of Castile - going to respond to all of this, knowing for sure, that to violate the pope's rule would undoubtedly incur the threat of ex-communication? Following Christopher Columbus' suggestion, they commissioned him to discover new lands beyond Portugal's geographical remit. Columbus initially thought that he could find a westward route to the Indies. Having studied the scriptural and legal basis for such an undertaking, he set out with a contract that would make him Spanish Admiral of any lands *en route*, that he would "discover and acquire."

When he came across already inhabited islands in the Caribbean, they were claimed for the Spanish crown, with Ferdinand and Isabella quickly

Figure 1. From a stamp engraved on copper by Th. De Bry, 1590: "Discovery of America, 12 May, 1492. Christopher Columbus erects the cross and baptizes the Isle of Guanahani by the Christian name of St. Salvador." In so doing he was exercising the protocols of the Doctrine of Discovery.

seeking papal endorsement regarding them. In 1493, Pope Alexander VI not only confirmed these discoveries, but he also issued the bull *Inter caetera divinai*, which granted Spain any other lands it might discover in the future, with the understanding that they were "not previously possessed by any Christian owner." (See Figure 1).

The Doctrine of Discovery arrives in the New World

Under international law, European monarchs now had gained ownership rights in the New World, giving them sovereignty and commercial rights over its people.

In 1493, Pope Alexander VI also issued *Inter Caetera II*, which drew a north-south line, approximately 300 miles off the Azores, granting Spain all the lands discovered or to be so, west of it. That was to be modified a year later in the Treaty of Tordesillas, as a means of reducing tensions between Spain and Portugal. In it, a new line was drawn up further west, giving Portugal discovery rights to a part of the New World, and what is now Brazil. That, simply put, is why today, Brazil is the only Portuguese-speaking country in South America!

Robert Miller drew on Anthony Pagden's book, "Lords of all the World: Ideologies of Empire in Spain, Britain and France c.1500-c.1800,"[11] to bring together four firmly established aspects of the Doctrine of Discovery by 1493:

> "First, the Church had the political and secular authority to grant to Christian kings some form of title and ownership rights in the lands of infidels. Second, European exploration and colonization were designed to assist the pope's guardianship duties over all the earthly flock, including infidels. Third, Spain and Portugal held exclusive rights over other European, Christian countries to explore and colonize the unknown parts of the entire world. Fourth, the mere sighting and discovery of new lands by Spain or Portugal in their respective spheres of influence and the symbolic possession of these lands by undertaking the Discovery rituals and formalities of possession, such as planting flags or leaving objects to

26

prove their presence, were sufficient to pass rights in these lands to the discovering European country."[12]

One of the most significant regulations regarding the actual outworking of Spain's natural law rights in the New World was a document developed by King Ferdinand in 1513, entitled the *Requerimiento*. It was to be read out to the natives, or at least in their hearing, even from the deck of a ship, before any hostilities or "just war" could have legally ensued. It informed them that their lands had been "donated" to Spain by the pope and that they should, therefore, acknowledge the Spanish King, the Church, and the gospel proclaimed to them by its priests. A refusal was enough for "just war" to be waged on them - which amounted to genocide by the conquistadores! (How's that for respecting and honouring the free will of the natives who didn't even know Spanish?)

At the time of Alexander VI's papal bull in 1493, England and France were both Catholic countries, and as such, they ran the risk of excommunication if they were to infringe Spanish or Portuguese Discovery rights. They could explore and trade but not claim any lands for the Crown or Church. This restriction would lead them to examine their legal position and develop a modified version of Discovery theory that enabled them to both explore and colonise in the New World.

In England, the legal scholars of Henry VII (a Catholic, who reigned from 1485-1509) were to put forward the idea that they would not violate a papal bull if their explorers limited themselves to only claiming lands that were not yet discovered by other Christian sovereignties. In the light of that, Henry VII granted a patent to the Italian navigator and explorer John Cabot and his son Sebastian in 1497. They were to set foot on American soil in Newfoundland, without the required Papal authority!

I shall pick up this trail again shortly, as we examine the Protestantisation of the Doctrine of Discovery: that came with Henry VIII and Elizabeth I. This was a political and, supposedly, doctrinal necessity to enable the growth of the British Empire, of which Ireland and the colonies in North America were initially a part.

Part III
Different roots, different fruits!

Thanks for hanging in there! You may well have been asking, "What has this got to do with Ireland?" As you will soon see - everything! Some would even say that Ireland, as England's oldest colony, is where they learnt the practice of Empire Expansion!!

So back to Ireland

To establish this, we need to go back in time, to have a look at some of the key points in Ireland's history, particularly regarding the actions of the Crown, as it sought to build an empire, before and after the Reformation. What follows is by no means an in-depth account, but rather a chronology of some significant events in our history. They are points where Satan was given a foothold to operate in Irish/English affairs. Every unresolved negative interaction in history (hence the significance of dates) verifies that. Such footholds do not disappear with time. They need to be named, understood and dealt with!

This current leg in my journey, started in Autumn 2019, when a friend of mine - Margaret Clarke (a member of the Transformations Ireland leadership team) – asked me about the image of the log, in the dream I had had many years before regarding the Beaver's Dam and the Ulster Covenant. She pointed out that the log had originally come from a tree and then asked if I had any thoughts regarding the nature of the tree and its root system. On reflection, I began to realise that for the past ten years of research for my book "*A Destiny Denied... A Dignity Restored*", I had inadvertently been researching into the same tree and its root system!

My findings in that research have served to both confirm and enlighten me further regarding many issues addressed in my first book "*Heal Not

28

Lightly," especially the relationship between Ireland and the UK. There is much in both of these books that the Church and governments in the USA and UK need to acknowledge and repent of!

Celtic Ireland

Before we move on to look at Ireland after the introduction of the English Crown and the influence of the papacy, let us take a brief look at Ireland - Celtic Ireland - prior to that. It is thought that from about 300AD, some knowledge of Christianity would have been available in Ireland through trading and other forms of contact with the Roman Empire in England. It is worth noting that the Roman Empire never conquered Ireland – though in more recent years Romano-British artifacts have been discovered on a coastal fortified site some fifteeen miles north of Dublin, dated to the late first or early second centuries[13] - this was before 330AD when Constantine embraced Christianity, and the Roman Church was formed.

Writing in 387AD, St. Chrysostom records that churches and altars were already to be found in Ireland, possibly brought here by Christians from Gaul. This is borne out by the words of Palladius, who was sent to Ireland in 431 by Pope Celestine, and specifically "to the Irish who believe in Christ," to ensure that the heresies of Pelagianism[14] did not get a hold here. This would have been around the same time as St. Patrick is thought to have come. According to the Irish annals for the fifth century, Patrick is thought to have arrived in Ireland in 432. Palladius's ministry centre was in Leinster, whereas Patrick's was predominantly in Ulster and Connacht and was considered more evangelistic in nature.

Irish writers chronicled that while St. Palladius preached in Ireland before St. Patrick, he was soon to be banished by the King of Leinster and returned to North Britain. According to Muirchu (who lived two centuries later) in the *Book of Armagh*, "God hindered him... and neither did those fierce and cruel men receive his doctrine readily, nor did he himself wish to spend time in a strange land but returned to him who sent him."[15]

St. Patrick

Patrick[16] has become known as the "Apostle of Ireland" and is identified by both Catholics and Protestants as Ireland's patron saint. He was never formally canonised by the Catholic Church, having lived before the regulations of the Catholic Church regarding this. Tradition regards him, not only as the founder of Christianity here but also as the first bishop of Armagh and Primate of Ireland. I, along with many others, would recognise that Patrick represents something of the 'good seed' of God's kingdom that predates the 'bad seed' of Christendom!

It is thought that he established churches in Ireland like the one in Armagh which had small enclosures in which groups of Christians - male, female and married, lived together - serving each other and ministering to the local population.

By the sixth century, a diocesan structure of the Irish Church evolved into a monastic hierarchy which was not ruled by Bishops. This produced a plethora of well-known figures such as Finnian, Brendan, and Colum Cille. By mid-sixth century, a network of missionary outreaches had developed, such as – Iona, Northumberland, Lindisfarne and out across Europe into France, Switzerland and Italy. Bangor Abbey, Co. Down, founded by Comgall around 558AD, is probably the most renowned of them, especially for its emphasis on worship (Latin hymns, prayers and antiphons).

In recent years there has been something of a revival in Celtic Spirituality. We talk of ancient wells of faith scattered across Ireland – places where foundational monasteries once existed – thin places! We see Ireland as something of a seed-bed of pre-Roman Christianity; the land of saints and scholars; a sending base for missionaries reaching out across Europe. Opening up these "blocked wells" has been a subject of increasing discussion and prayer for our land in these days.

Anglo-Saxons (c. 410-1066)

They were a Germanic people who began to arrive in Britain in the fifth century from the North Sea coastlands of Europe, following the collapse of the Roman Empire in 410AD. Historians are not quite sure why the

Anglo-Saxons came to Britain. Some sources say that the Saxon warriors were invited to come to the area now known as England, to help keep out invaders from Scotland and Ireland. Another possible reason for coming may have been due to their land often flooding, making it difficult to grow crops, so they were looking for new places to settle down and farm. The name England comes from the Saxon word 'Angle-Land.' Their influence lasted until 1066, with the coming of the Normans.

Towards the end of the sixth century, Pope Gregory the Great sent Augustine to evangelise the "Angles." His mission was centered at Canterbury where he became Archbishop in 597. The Irish Celtic missionaries did likewise, basing themselves at Iona. In 644AD, what had become an uneasy coexistence between the Celtic and Roman Churches came to a head at the Council of Whitby in Northumbria, where differences of opinion regarding which date Easter should be celebrated, were aired! Up to that point, both Churches had been using different formats to decide it.

The bottom line of the dispute was, however, the issue of authority. While Rome did not want to insist on absolute uniformity at this stage, neither did the Celts want to be a wholly separate Church, but there clearly were tensions. Ultimately, who had the authority to determine the means of calculating Easter? Rome clearly felt that it had. Back in 314AD, at the Council of Arles, it had been agreed that Easter ought to be celebrated on the same day throughout the Church. Based on the belief that Petrine authority was invested in the pope and his representative, Augustine, Canterbury's position would win the day.

The Council of Whitby was a turning point in the history of the Celtic Church and in relations between the English and Irish Churches, for two reasons. Firstly, it marked the beginning of the decline in the influence of the Celtic Church in Britain. Secondly, Canterbury was emerging to become the seat of English Christianity.

Whitby also foreshadowed a growing complexity in relationships, not only among the Irish but between the Irish and English kings, the English Church and the papacy. In particular, the question of the jurisdiction of Canterbury would resurface throughout the coming centuries. That not only created resentment in the Irish Church but, at times, it led Irish political and ecclesiastical leaders into making unlikely alliances to maintain or achieve the Irish Church's independence from Canterbury. This is something that was going to be eventually challenged, as it would be seen as something aberrant by the papacy.

Reform within the Catholic Church

By the middle of the 11th century the Church throughout Europe – including Ireland - was considered to be in much need of reform. Many of the clergy were married, held hereditary offices and others held high offices without belonging to a holy order. Early in the 12th century, more than one English primate wrote, encouraging the Irish Kings to initiate a reform programme in the Church. This led in 1101 to a Synod being held in Cashel, which forbade simony (the buying or selling of ecclesiastical privileges, e.g., Church Offices) and the ordaining of lay abbots and clerics to marry. Ten years later, yet another Synod held in Ráth Breasil, moved the church from being a monastic to a diocesan/parish-based church. This could be seen as part of the centralising, hierarchical control of the papacy, which had its roots in the birth of Christendom.

Pre-Reformation Britain and Ireland

The Normans
They were descendants of the Vikings from Scandinavia, who had settled in an area of northern France, now known as Normandy, since the 9th century. They were particularly known for their martial prowess, and through their alignment with the papacy, they became part of the European forces that helped to establish the new Crusader states in Palestine. They had also proven themselves to be adaptable and ready to integrate with their conquered peoples, which was soon to be evidenced after their invasion of England and later in Ireland.

A significant expression of papal authority in Britain was established in 1066 when William the Conqueror (Duke of Normandy) came to England with papal assent to defeat the Anglo-Saxon King of England, Harold Godwinson, at the Battle of Hastings.

This was the beginning of the Norman conquest of England. This assent took the form of a Papal ring; the Standard of St. George; an edict to modernise the old Anglo-Saxon Church and a flag bearing the Papal

Figure 2. A section of the Bayeaux Tapestry showing a flag bearing the Papal Insignia.

Insignia carried by Count Eustace of Bologna – shown on the Bayeux Tapestry, (Fig.2). This is an early expression of the developing Doctrine of Discovery protocols.

They would become the first to recognise the jurisdiction of Canterbury over the island of Ireland. Indeed, the Archbishops of Armagh and Dublin were for a time consecrated by the Archbishop of Canterbury. The Synod of Kells in 1152, brought about the re-organisation of the Irish Church into Roman-styled dioceses, with it regaining its independence from Canterbury, and Armagh being recognised as the ecclesiastical capital of Ireland. In these political and ecclesiastical manoeuvres, the seeds of the Norman invasion were sown, inevitably bringing with them, internal power struggles. Their intermarriage with the Irish would lead to their integration into Irish society.

Ireland had, for some time, been moving towards accepting a strong central monarchy, but with no properly defined system or means of doing so, rival Gaelic kings contended for the honour. During one of the many episodes of wrangling over the high-kingship with churchmen as well as soldiers taking sides, Dermott Mac Murrough, King of Leinster, was ousted from power following an attack in 1166 by an ally of the High King Rory O'Connor. Dermott fled to England to look for support. Landing in Bristol, he was advised to seek out Henry II, who permitted Dermott to recruit from among his subjects. This brought him into contact with the Anglo-Norman warrior, Strongbow (Richard FitzGilbert de Clare, the Earl of Pembroke), who agreed to assist him.

In 1169, using an earlier authorisation from the English Pope Adrian IV in 1155 – the papal bull, *Laudibiliter*[17] - Strongbow, landed with his army in Co. Wexford and defeated Dermott's enemies (see Henry II, pg. 35). They moved quickly to impose themselves on the native Irish and captured Waterford and Dublin. When Dermott died the following year, Strongbow was to succeed him as King of Leinster. Fearing that Strongbow might establish an independent kingship, Henry II came to Ireland in 1171 to consolidate his rule, though internal feuding between Norman overlords and Gaelic kings would continue. Six years later the English Crown's claim to have Lordship over Ireland was conferred by Henry onto his son John.

The English Crown in Ireland

What follows now is a series of short cameos, pictures of the English Crown's colonial expansion into Ireland, with some unavoidable overlaps between those on the throne and historical events. As the Irish were the ones being oppressed, these will have a predominantly Irish perspective regarding England's negative role here, though, as you will see, atrocities were also carried out between the clans. As I have already mentioned in Part I, any such negative interactions could be described as Satan being given footholds of his kingdom purposes in Ireland against that of God's Kingdom.

Throughout the Middle Ages, only two other English Kings set foot in Ireland – John, and following a long gap in time, Richard II. Even with the investment of more people coming from England to live here, absolute control never happened. While English laws were never fully enforced, hence Ireland certainly never became a "little England", it nevertheless produced a degree of animosity - if we are under English rule, why do we not have all of its benefits?

In a sense, military conquest would have been relatively easy, but instead, by inhabiting the lands they took, they established a *conquest by colonisation* process that radically changed the course of history here. Economically, they utilised the lands with English farming techniques and recruited the Irish along with an increasing flow of English as farm labourers; new towns sprang up; larger castles were built and trade, both internal and foreign, increased.

Irish resistance, nevertheless, was felt from the start by the settler-colonisers. Initially, this resistance arose more out of local concerns than national ones, but it would ensure the survival of some of the more important native dynasties.

Henry II (r. 1154-89)
He was William the Conqueror's great-grandson and as I have mentioned, he came to Ireland in 1171, having been given, through the *Laudibiliter*, papal authority from Pope Adrian IV. Chosen by God to civilise the barbaric savages, it granted him the right to invade Ireland and govern it by portioning out swathes of land to his loyal subjects and also bring the semi-autonomous Irish Church under Papal authority. It was an early articulation of the dynamics being developed by the papacy which would become known as the Doctrine of Discovery.

This was a very significant action, as he was the first English King to set foot in Ireland, with full Papal authority. It was, I believe, the entry point for the "empire spirit" of Christendom, into Ireland. Its people, politics and Church - would never be the same! Both king and pope, in a sense needed each other, as they were both in empire expansion mode: Henry sought to bring Ireland under his domain for political reasons and the papacy was seeking to exercise its control as the supreme authority, even over the Crowns of Europe for spiritual and political reasons. That twin role of the Catholic Church was to become a dominant influential force in Ireland.

Following the Reformation, the oppression of Catholicism by the English Crown continued, e.g., the introduction of Penal Laws. This meant that freedom from the Crown would become an important component in the growing idea of national and religious freedom.

While Henry, and his successors would claim Lordship of Ireland, in reality this was never fully realised. Most of it, known as Gaelic

Ireland, would continue to be under the control of Irish chiefdoms, that recurrently warred against their Anglo-Norman neighbours.

Through time, many of the English leaders in Ireland would die without leaving male heirs. Alongside that, many colonisers had integrated themselves into Irish cultural life, something the more formal, conservative members of colonial society looked upon with disdain. The Statutes of Kilkenny in 1366, was an unsuccessful attempt at reversing this. It nevertheless showed the strength of Gaelic culture that persisted.

Other English monarchs would maintain their presence in Ireland via landlords - their colonial administration.

It would take approximately another four hundred years after Henry II's death before the ever-evolving DOD would appear in a Protestantised format in the reign of Queen Elizabeth I (1558), as she, with the aid of Lord Chief Justice Coke, granted Charters for the colonisation of North America. What is key here, for us to grasp, is that the DOD traversed the Reformation.

King John (r. 1199-1216)
In 1177, five years after Strongbow had died, Henry II appointed his son John, to become the future ruler of Ireland. He was just 11 years old!

On his return to England from Ireland in December 1185, a gift from the pope was waiting for him - a golden coronet embellished with peacock feathers known as a 'tufa.' This was a highly symbolic gift associated with a military conquest and dated back to the Byzantium emperors. It was an affirmation from the pope regarding John's presence in Ireland.

Indeed, he was with a fair degree of skill, able to build around himself a group of people who were set to become the future administrative elite. In 1185, families such as the Burghs, the Verduns and the Butlers (formerly Theobald Walter, his butler) were deliberately recruited into Irish service. Over the ensuing centuries these families would be the mainstay of England's administration here.

He also did not hold back from exercising his military responsibilities, building castles at Lismore, Tybroughney and Ardfinnan, from which he could exploit rivalries between the native dynasties in the southwest of Ireland. It was here, that John learned how to manipulate the clear tensions between colonial and native elites, stirring up tensions between them. Another part of his armoury was his use of headhunting the native Irish, collecting the heads of dead enemies as trophies. Reporting on his Irish expedition in 1185, he wrote "A hundred heads sent to Dublin." Clearly fear was a weapon to be used! It did nothing for future Irish-English relationships!

In an article by Nicholas Vincent, Professor of Medieval History at the University of East Anglia, he wrote about Ireland being a land at war with itself,

> "From the beginning, this was a settlement founded upon bloodshed and expropriation. As in England after the conquest of 1066, colonisers were massively outnumbered by natives. But by contrast to Anglo-Saxon England, Ireland remained a land deeply divided between warring sub-kingdoms. It lacked anything comparable to the administrative sophistication of the Anglo-Saxons. Nor had the Irish themselves suffered the sort of defeat inflicted by the battle of Hastings in 1066 to persuade them of their ultimate doom. There were the seeds here of future violence and paranoia.

> "A vast solitude" inhabited by "wild and ferocious barbarians" was how one English monk described Ireland in the 1170s. Even 50 years later, another English visitor reported it as a land divided by "a most evil and dangerous frontier between English and Irish", still only a small part of it established as a "land of peace."[18]

Henry III (r. 1216-72)
Though he never set foot in Ireland, it was important to him, not only as a means of royal revenue but it also supplied estates that could be conferred upon his supporters. Throughout the 1240s, following the deaths of some of the barons, he had to redistribute Irish lands to some of their successors, which enabled him to maintain an English presence. At the same time, this invariably led to increased harassment from the local Irish leaders.

In 1254, Henry granted Ireland to his son, Edward, on the condition that it would never be separated from the Crown.[19]

Edward's 1 – III. (1272 - 1377)
Ireland does not appear to have featured much during their reigns, as they were mostly involved in internal affairs and a preoccupation with Scotland, Wales and France. Nevertheless, the internal struggles between Irish and Anglo-Norman overlords continued.

Richard II (r. 1377- deposed in 1399)
He visited Ireland twice during his reign (1394 and 1399) and sought to financially bolster up the presence of the colonists here, even though large swathes of the land were still not under direct English control. His successors were to pull back on this, leaving some of the powerful families like the Fitzgeralds and Butlers to fill the gap by representing the Crown and defending the English presence. This, however, was not overly successful as they had become "too Irish", much to the disdain of the settlers in the area known as the Pale - land between Dublin and Dundalk, in which many sought to maintain their Englishness and their connection with London.

Henry V (r. 1413-22)
He had been in Ireland with Richard II, but beyond that, he does not appear to have significantly engaged with it during his reign. He is better known and celebrated as one of the greatest warrior kings of medieval England, especially featuring in the War of the Roses and the 100 Years War with France.

Henry VI (r. 1422-61; 1470-71)
Like his predecessors, he was concerned with internal affairs – Scotland, Wales and Europe. He tried to maintain England's hold on Ireland through a series of ports, stretching south from Carrickfergus going around as far as Galway, aware of the possibility of "back-door" offensives from Europe into England.

Henry VII (r. 1485-1509)
Throughout the 16th century, things were to come to a head in Ireland under the reigns of Henry VII and Henry VIII - with disastrous effects.

Ireland represented a huge challenge to Henry VII's belief in a strong monarchical rule. During the War of the Roses, Ireland had primarily sided with the Yorkists and so, as a Lancastrian, Henry had little support from them. We should not be surprised then, that Henry VII had to develop a different approach to ruling over what was one of his most difficult regions.

In 1485, he used an already proven method of governance by appointing a Lord Lieutenant, whose authority was exercised through a Lord Deputy in Ireland. However, outside of the Pale, the real power in the majority of Ireland continued to lie with the chieftains and the two most powerful clans, the Butler and Geraldine families. The latter held many important government positions including Lord Deputy and Chancellor of Ireland. It was only in 1492, after the Earl of Kildare, leader of the Geraldine family, recognised Perkin Warbeck (who claimed to be the younger son of Edward IV, a pretender to the throne and considered by some as the rightful king of England), that they were all stripped of their posts.

Following that, Henry tried to impose an English form of government in Ireland by appointing his young son, Prince Henry, as Lord Lieutenant of Ireland. The position of Lord Deputy was then given to one of his trusted advisors, Sir Edward Poynings, who introduced a Law whereby he sought to bring the Irish chieftains under control by trying to assert monarchical authority in Ireland.

Poyning's Law (1494)

Through it, any independent authority that the Irish Parliament believed it had was removed. The Irish Parliament could only be called by the King; any future legislation or possible new laws had to have the King's prior agreement and any laws passed in England were to be automatically applied to Ireland. This reinforced the authority, and therefore the power, of the king.

In the long term, such actions were counter-productive. The King's Council looked at Ireland with English eyes, which meant that any Irish legislation would be influenced by English ideas, devoid of any real understanding of Irish conditions. He was trying to persuade the Irish leaders to align themselves on the side of centralised government and law and order. The only other alternative was a militaristic government that would enforce law and order.

This would ultimately proved too costly for Henry to maintain, and so he reverted to ruling through the chieftains. So, the Earl of Kildare was reinstated as Lord Deputy of Ireland in 1496. He became so powerful that he was named "the uncrowned King of Ireland." It may not have been the solution Henry wanted, but it was a practical one that served the purpose of relieving him of most of his Irish problems throughout the rest of his reign.

Henry VIII (r. 1509-47)

As he had no children, and the pope wouldn't permit his divorce, he responded by setting up his own church, The Church of England, which enabled him to remarry. While he was still very Catholic in his thinking, ex-communication did not seriously bother him. This also meant that British Empire expansion was now on the cards and things in Ireland were to have a dramatic turn in events:

- The Irish nobility ruled the area within the Pale – known as the Colony.
- The rest of Ireland was under the control of the ruling families. Their religious loyalty to Rome meant that their loyalty to the Crown was minimal.
- In 1534 Thomas, Lord Offaly, son of the 9th Earl of Kildare, renounced his allegiance to the Crown and laid siege on Dublin. This insurrection was quickly put down when Sir William Skeffington landed with a force from England. Following Thomas's surrender, he was executed. This put an end to the power of the Kildare family; his affairs were now firmly under English officials and administrators.
- Offaly's attempt at rallying the Irish in a "Catholic crusade" would introduce religious adversity, into Irish politics for the first time.
- Henry went on to impose his Reformation by force, creating further religious division.
- During 1536-37, a now subservient Irish Parliament passed statutes regarding the Reformation, which brought them in line with England and Wales.
- Notably in 1542, Henry VIII was declared King of Ireland by the Irish parliament through the Crown of Ireland Act.
- He also had the title, of the head of the "Church in Ireland" conferred on him.
- By 1547, Henry's supremacy was accepted by all the main players in his realm. Monasteries would also be dissolved, though in Ireland

this was harder to enforce outside of the Pale. The Irish nevertheless saw the Reformation as a sign of English Protestant supremacy over them.

The Reformation - 1533 onwards

The Reformation came to Ireland as part of Henry VIII's programme of breaking with the papacy. With it, Church and state institutions were more closely linked to the monarchy. In 1534, Parliament passed the Act of Supremacy which made Henry VIII the supreme head of the Church of England. Any act of allegiance to the papacy was considered treasonous because the papacy claimed both spiritual and political power over its followers. These powers were now conferred on the Protestant Crown.

In 1541, he gave Ireland the constitutional status of a kingdom. In so doing, he was saying that Ireland was no longer under papal control! As I have already mentioned, England could not "do empire" in North America because it had not been given papal authority to do so. Nevertheless, everything points to the fact that it understood the DOD by the fact that it knew what it couldn't do, for fear of ex-communication. Under King Henry VIII all that was to change, not only for North America but also for Ireland! What we need to realise is, that the "spirit of empire" by crossing over into the Reformation, sadly added a sectarian dynamic into the equation.

Henry's son, **Edward VI** (1547–53), at the age of nine, formally established Protestantism as the state religion. His reign only lasted for six years and his principal reform, the Act of Uniformity 1549, had much less impact in Ireland than in England. This, the first Act of its kind, was an attempt at making religious worship uniform across England and its territories. Because different branches of the Church were not in agreement with some of its content, further modifications would eventually follow. It was also during his reign that Archbishop Cranmer wrote the Book of Common Prayer.

Mary I (Bloody Mary) (r. 1553-58)
The daughter of Henry VIII and Catherine of Aragon. As a devout Catholic, she energetically attempted to enforce a comprehensive conversion of England back to Catholicism. The country was plunged

into a bitter blood bath, with many including the Protestant bishops, Latimer, Ridley and Archbishop Cranmer being burnt at the stake. This is why she is remembered as Bloody Mary. Her reign also coincided with the Counter-Reformation.

The Counter-Reformation

Between 1545 and 1563, The Council of Trent was convened by Pope Paul III in response to the Protestant Reformation. It clarified most of its doctrines and teachings that were contested by Protestantism and played a key role in revitalising the Roman Catholic Church in most of Europe. While the Reformation may have been successfully implemented in England and Wales, it failed in large part in Ireland, at least outside of Ulster and The Pale, due to the vigorous and successful Counter-Reformation. As the Catholic religion had been so deeply rooted within the culture prior to the Reformation in Ireland, it made it very hard to replace it with any new expression. Added to that, the tensions between the Old English (Catholic local elites) and English Protestant rule in Ireland would cause their loyalty towards the English monarchy to diminish.

Because of military intervention, which led to the lands of the old elites being reduced, rebellion against the new settlers and the English rulers was inevitable. The seeds for sectarianism in Ireland were truly being sown. It made Ireland, arguably, the greatest anomaly in the progress of the European Protestant Reformation as the only country not to follow the religion of its ruler.[20]

Elizabeth I (r. 1558-1603)
The daughter of Henry VIII and Anne Boleyn.

1559. Following Mary's death, the Act of Supremacy re-established the Church of England's independence from Rome and Elizabeth took on the title of the Supreme Governor of the Church of England.

1560. The Irish Act of Supremacy was passed which reasserted the position of the Anglican Church of Ireland as the state church. Attendance at Church of Ireland services became obligatory; anyone who took office in the Irish church or government was required to take the Oath of Supremacy; those who refused to attend, whether Roman Catholics or Protestant nonconformists, could be fined and physically punished by the civil powers.

In 1570, the papal bull, *Regnans in Excelsis* was issued. In it, Queen Elizabeth I was excommunicated, declared as a pretender, and it called on her subjects to disobey her. In Ireland this not only removed any sense of Catholic loyalty to the English Crown, but it also hardened the Government's attitude towards Catholicism. Roman Catholics were increasingly seen as a threat to the security of the state.

Elizabeth I in Ireland

Had she been successful in winning over the Catholic local elites in Ireland, the rest of the population would probably have fallen into line and the Reformation could have been a success. As we know, that didn't happen, and as a result, a steady and deepening schism between the Old English and English was to develop. In Ireland the Old English were side-lined to make room for the seemingly more loyal New English, who began to challenge the dominance of the elite, lead to a growing bitterness arising among them.

England was aware that there was always the possibility of Catholic European nations using Ireland as a back door for an attack. This was not unfounded, as in July 1580 a small papally sponsored invasion force of Italian and Spanish soldiers landed at Smerwick on the County Kerry coast (for more information see below under Rebellion in 1580).

During the Munster uprising (1579-1583), known as the Desmond Rebellions, widespread civilian deaths were recorded. Right across the province, Elizabeth's forces deployed a scorched earth policy: harvests were burned, cattle seized and famine ensued, resulting in approximately 30,000 deaths. It must be said that this was not all one-sided, as there were many retaliatory atrocities committed against the English soldiers. Throughout the Tudor period, such activities against the Irish continued without intervention from London. By 1583, the rising across the south of Ireland was brought under control by the much-favoured subject of the Queen, Sir Walter Raleigh. Large-scale plantation was introduced as England sought to permanently solve the issue.

Furthermore, Raleigh's half-brother, Sir Humphrey Gilbert also served in Ireland during the plantation process (1566-72). Following the assassination of Shane O'Neill in 1567 he was appointed a Governor of Ulster.

Sir Richard Grenville, a cousin of Raleigh, was also part of the forces seeking to quell the Irish rebellion and colonise. Like Raleigh and Gilbert, he was also known for his ruthlessness.

All of these men were involved in the early colonisation of North America, often dealing with the Native Americans in a similar fashion. Parallels have been made regarding Ireland and the American colonies throughout the 1600-1700s. Catholic Irish and Native Americans were both seen as "savages"!

Rebellion in 1580

Munster was ruled by the Earl of Desmond, an Irish Roman Catholic nobleman. However, in 1580, a rebellion against Queen Elizabeth began in Munster. It was hoped that help would come from the Catholic king of Spain to defeat Queen Elizabeth. When the Earl of Desmond failed to put down the rebellion he was called a traitor by the agents of the Crown, resulting in his estate lands being set on fire and his tenants being killed. His castles were also taken. Having escaped, the Earl of Desmond was hunted down and killed and approximately 300,000 acres of land in Munster taken over by the English crown.

That same year, the Queen's new deputy, Lord Grey, led an English fleet of ships into the bay of Smerwick, to lay siege to the fort being defended by six hundred Spanish, Italian and Irish soldiers. The siege was broken after three days, followed by their surrender. In complete disregard for the rules of war, Sir Walter Raleigh, as an Officer of the Crown, was given the command to carry out their execution. For services rendered to the crown Raleigh was in receipt of 40,000 acres of land. Little wonder that such barbarous actions of the English in Ireland did nothing to help English-Irish relations for centuries to come!

The Flight of the Earls (September 1607)

In what became known as the 'The Nine Years War' (1594-1603), chiefs from the O'Neil and O'Donnell clans resisted the English armies that were sent to enforce control in Ulster. Even though the chiefs won many battles they had hoped to get further assistance from Queen Elizabeth's rival, Philip of Spain.

A major English defeat at the Battle of the Yellow Ford and the rebellion spreading to Munster only added to the concern over possible Spanish intervention. Following a number of appeals from the Irish to Philip of Spain, it finally arrived in the Autumn of 1601. Unfortunately the Spanish fleet arrived in Co. Cork, not Ulster! This meant that the Gaelic forces had a long March south to connect up with them, only to be defeated by Lord Mountjoy's army at Kinsale, Cork.'

In 1603, Hugh O'Neill signed a treaty at Mellifont which brought an end to the War. They were told that they could keep their lands if they promised to live according to English feudal rather than Irish Breton law. However, due to mounting pressure, Hugh O'Neill, along with others of the Ulster Gaelic aristocracy, left for the continent in what is infamously known as The Flight of the Earls. Queen Elizabeth died that year and a new ruling family called the Stuarts came to the throne in England.

James I of England and VI of Scotland (r. 1603-25)
Because Queen Elizabeth I had died, both unmarried and childless, the English crown passed to her cousin James VI, King of Scotland who was her next available heir. As a result, in 1603, England and Scotland were to share the same monarch, in what became known as the Union of the Crowns. He also became known as James I of England.

His reign saw the continued rise of the Puritan movement in England. It began during the reign of Queen Elizabeth I and it continued to clash with the authorities of the Church of England. In 1620 some of the Non-conformist Puritans (the Pilgrim Fathers) set sail for America in their ship The Mayflower.

In Ireland in 1605 a Proclamation was made against religious toleration. It ordered all of the laity to only attend services of the established church. Fines were issued to those who did not comply, this especially affected the Old English landowners and townsmen. All priests were ordered to leave Ireland.

Alienation between the Anglicans and Puritans was to continue up to the end of King Charles I's reign and the beginning of the English Civil War (1642-51) and the brief rule of the Puritan Lord Protector of England Oliver Cromwell (1653-58). Puritanism in Ireland and America was to have devastating consequences for the native peoples of both lands.

The Plantation of Ulster (1609-1690)

It was during James I's reign, with the Flight of the Earls, that plans were drawn up for the plantation of lands in Ulster that had now come under the Crown's ownership.

According to Wikipedia,[21]

> "Most of the settlers (or planters) came from southern Scotland and northern England... the official plantation began in 1609... comprised [of] an estimated half a million acres (2,000 km^2) of arable land in counties Armagh, Cavan, Fermanagh, Tyrone, Tyrconnell and Londonderry. Land in counties Antrim, Down and Monaghan was privately colonised with the king's support.
>
> Among those involved in planning and overseeing the plantation were King James, the Lord Deputy of Ireland, Arthur Chichester, and the Attorney-General for Ireland, John Davies. They saw the plantation as a means of controlling, anglicising and "civilising" Ulster. The province was almost wholly Gaelic, Catholic and rural, and had been... resistant to English control.
>
> The plantation was also meant to sever Gaelic Ulster's links with the Gaelic Highlands of Scotland. The colonists were required to be English-speaking, Protestant, and loyal to the king... The Scottish settlers were mostly Presbyterian Lowlanders [Dissenters] and the English mostly members of the Church of England. Although some 'loyal' natives were granted land, the native Irish reaction to the plantation was generally hostile, and native writers bewailed what they saw as the decline of Gaelic society and the influx of foreigners.
>
> The Plantation of Ulster was the biggest of the Plantations of Ireland. It led to the founding of many of Ulster's towns and created a lasting Ulster Protestant

community in the province with ties to Britain. It also resulted in many of the native Irish losing their land and led to ethnic and sectarian conflict, notably in the Irish rebellion of 1641."

Plantation was also implemented in other parts of Ireland, for example, Wexford and the Midlands, with the similar intent of establishing communities loyal to the Protestant Crown. Initially, James I appeared to be lenient with the Catholic laity and focused on persecuting the Church hierarchy, especially the Jesuits and seminarians. However, events in England, such as the Gunpowder Plot, were to change that. In Ireland, the Gaelic Irish and Old English were to increasingly feel the backlash. Not surprisingly, a political movement would rise in opposition, with the Catholic Church to the fore!

Settlement, however, was slower than anticipated. Undertakers (people who agreed to oversee the 'planting' of British settlers on the estates they were given), preferred Irish tenants, as they could exact higher rents from them and they weren't given any security of tenure through a lease. In 1610 County Coleraine was excluded from the scheme, with settlement there designated to a group of London livery companies, who were initially reticent in backing the scheme. The County's name was changed to Londonderry and a walled city, of the same name, was built. The new social structures would be strictly adhered to, with Catholics reduced to living in the low-lying, marshy area known as the Bogside.

Despite many incentives, the Planter population was still sparsely distributed. So, for some time, it would require an Irish presence to make the project financially workable. It is understood that by 1622 only thirteen thousand colonists had taken up grants for land. It would take nearly twenty years for that number to grow to over thirty thousand. Neil Hegarty, in *The Story of Ireland*,[22] gives us further insights:

> "Across the Plantation counties, the settlers from the very outset adopted an embattle outlook, inhabiting both physically walled settlements and fortresses of the mind. Habitually they worked the fields with a weapon to hand; and tales spread of refugee Irish lurking in the woods and uplands. At times ready to seize the

opportunity to wreak havoc on the planted towns and tilled fields. Gaelic Ireland was imagined intensely by the settlers: brooding beyond their walls, disposed, unsettled and threatening... Ultimately, planter numbers would swell – augmented not solely by English men and women but increasingly by settlers crossing the North Channel from Scotland...

These new colonists were predominantly (but not wholly) Dissenters: Presbyterians whose cultural attitudes were already profoundly adversarial, having been the object of religious persecution in Scotland itself, and who arrived in Ireland to find themselves once again on the wrong side of a High Church regime. They came determined both to claim their new land of Ulster from popery and barbarism and to maintain their own distinct faith and identity... These newcomers carried with them a religious culture that, with its overtones of egalitarianism and democracy, was wholly different from any that had hitherto existed in Ireland: there was little sense of hierarchy among the Dissenters, no caste of bishops ready to triangulate the relationship between God and the flock. They brought too a fierce certainty that they were a chosen people and that Ulster was to be their promised land... "

Charles I (r. 1625-49)
While he may have still held to the principle of the divine right of Kings he showed no strength of commitment to Protestantism. Also having a Catholic princess as his consort, would not have endeared him to an increasingly Puritan Parliament, which indirectly, led to the outbreak of the English Civil War in 1642. His authority in Scotland was also weakened as Calvinism gained prominence there. In 1638, in opposition to Reforms, the Presbyterian Church of Scotland led its people into signing the National Covenant, uniting them in patriotic fervour against the Crown. Something that was emulated here in Ireland in 1912 by the Presbyterian Church.

This culminated in a four-year-long war, which came to an end following the defeat of Charles's Royalist forces (which included many Irish

Catholics) by Oliver Cromwell's New Model Army. Following Charles's capture and imprisonment, he was tried for treason by The House of Commons. Having been found guilty he was condemned to death and was beheaded on 30th January, 1649. Following this, the British monarchy was abolished and a republic called the Commonwealth of England was declared.

The Irish Rebellion of 1641

Two possible reasons have been given as to what triggered this:

- It was a pre-emptive strike by Catholic Ireland to overthrow the Protestant regime in Ireland.
- It was the result of long-standing grievances associated with the Ulster Plantation.

It was probably a mixture of both of these, along with smouldering resentment, which eventually boiled over into the vicious attacks on the Protestant settlers, which led to a large number of fatalities.

The rebellion of 1641 would have ripple effects lasting for years, as it spread to other areas of Ireland, with the Old English co-religionists joining in. At one point, Protestant dominance in Ulster was in danger of being eradicated, when in 1646 Owen Roe O'Neill led the Catholics in a famous victory at the battle of Benburb (County Tyrone), during which the main Protestant army in Ireland was decimated. It has been estimated that approximately 12,000 Protestants died, many from the cold or disease, having been expelled from their homes in winter, with approximately 3,000 returning to England. Recent research has shown that 1,250 Protestants were killed in County Armagh during the early months of the rebellion.[23] While in Kinard, Co. Tyrone most of the British families there were also murdered.[24]

However, the rebellion did not stop migration of the British and Scots, which resumed after the rebellion. By 1659 Planters accounted for almost a third of the population in the province. The population in Ulster would also be geographically divided, those of Irish extraction lived on the poorer quality marginal lands, while the British community were settled on the better agricultural land.

49

The Ulster Plantation set in place the long-term division of the province into Protestant and Catholic communities. The massacres of 1641 left permanent and deep scars in the corporate memory of both. One atrocity, which is burned deeply into the Protestant psyche to this day, took place in Portadown, in November 1641. Under the command of Toole McCann, a hundred British Protestant settlers were forced off the bridge into the River Bann, with anyone who tried to escape being shot.

The wars of the 1640s would also serve to strengthen the position of the Presbyterian Church in Ireland. However, by the 18th century, Penal legislation, which was designed to establish conformity to the Church of Ireland by undermining Catholicism, also had the added effect of consolidating the allegiance of Presbyterians (seen as non-Conformists) against the Crown. This would ultimately lead to many of them emigrating to the North American colonies.

Oliver Cromwell, Lord Protector (1653–58)
Cromwell was born in 1599 at Huntingdon, Cambridgeshire, the son of a small landowner. In 1629 he entered Parliament, where he was actively involved in the events which lead to the Civil War. He was also a member of a 'Special Commission' that tried and condemned Charles I to death, having been unable to successfully reach an agreement with him regarding constitutional change in the Government. Following that he declared Britain a republic (also known as The Commonwealth), of which he became its Lord Protector.

Cromwell was passionately opposed to the Catholic Church. The Rebellion of 1641 did nothing to abate that.

The Cromwellian War in Ireland (1649–53)

In August 1649, Cromwell's troops sailed to Ireland to meet with strong resistance in Drogheda. As a result, Cromwell ordered his soldiers "in the heat of the action" not to "spare any that were in arms in the town." Despite laying their arms down (in the hopes of being taken as prisoners of war), many were executed in cold blood. This was in breach of the contemporary rules of war at the time.

Regarding his attack on Drogheda, Cromwell wrote on 16 September

1649, "I believe we put to the sword the whole number of the defenders. I do not think 30 of the whole number escaped with their lives; those that did are in safe custody for Barbados..." Cromwell listed the dead as including, "many inhabitants" of Drogheda, in his report to Parliament. Hugh Peters, an officer on Cromwell's council of war, gave the total loss of life as 3,552, of whom about 2,800 were soldiers, meaning that between 700-800 civilians were killed. Irish Clerical sources in the 1660s claimed that 4,000 civilians had died and denounced the sacking as "unparalleled savagery and treachery beyond any slaughterhouse." *(https://en.wikipaedia.org/wiki/Seige_of_Drogheda).*

In this article, we further read that Cromwell defended his actions at Drogheda, as revenge for the massacre of Protestant settlers in Ulster in 1641. In a letter to the Speaker of the House of Commons, he justified it as follows:

> "I am persuaded that this is a righteous judgment of God on these barbarous wretches, who have imbrued their hands with so much innocent blood; and that it will tend to prevent the effusion of blood for the future, which are satisfactory grounds for such actions which cannot otherwise but work remorse and regret."

In October he also besieged Wexford, where another massacre took place, with 2,000 Irish troops and approximately 1,500 civilians being killed and most of the town burned down. Following this, soldiers were sent to Ulster while he went on to besiege Kilkenny, Clonmel (its initial resistance was to cost him the lives of 2000 soldiers), New Ross and Carlow. He was to return to England in May 1650 due to an uprising in Scotland. The Irish campaign was to continue under different leadership for nearly three years, though long sieges and guerrilla warfare were to cost them many lives. Following the conquest of Ireland, Roman Catholicism was banned. Any captured priests were killed.

A new act of Parliament, the Adventurer's Act, enabled him to reward those who helped him defeat the Irish, with a portion of confiscated lands.

Catholic Ireland was eventually subdued in 1653, following a catalogue of massacres and atrocities being committed by both sides. It has also been documented that Irish prisoners were sent to Barbados as slaves/ indentured servants (their actual status is a debate for another day!).

Following his death in 1658, his son Richard Cromwell was appointed as the second Lord Protector of England, Scotland and Ireland. Lacking the military prowess of his father, he was 'encouraged' after just nine months, to relinquish his post as Lord Protector. He went into exile in France until he returned to England in 1680.

The Restoration

May 1660 marks the date of the restoration of the Crown in England. Charles II became king and the bishops were restored to Parliament, enabling the establishing of a strict Anglican orthodoxy.

Charles II (r. 1660–85)
"Charles's own priority in 1660 was the restoration of the Church of Ireland, and this was accomplished expeditiously through a complete set of appointments to vacant bishoprics and the passage of a new Act of Uniformity (1666). Those who hoped for a policy of accommodation with the Presbyterian community were disappointed. A three-tier system emerged in which only members of the Protestant Established Church, who constituted perhaps 40 percent of the Protestant community, enjoyed full privileges. Presbyterians, who accounted for about one-third of Irish Protestants and whose numbers increased steadily with continued migration from Scotland to Ulster, were subject to religious and civil disabilities, as were other Protestant dissenters. In practice, they were allowed to worship freely, but their marriages and the legitimacy of their children were not recognised and their conscientious refusal to take an oath acknowledging the king as the supreme governor of the church excluded them from appointment to public office. Catholics, were tolerated at the Crown's discretion...

At the insistence of Protestants in Ireland, who recognised that the preservation of the land settlement depended upon the retention of political power, Catholics ceased to be admitted to membership in the Irish parliament. The right to vote was not withheld, but Catholic voting strength was greatly reduced by the loss of property and by a related shift of control in the towns, which had become Protestant enclaves.

The… mainstay of the settlement was the control of military force. The standing army, at between 5,000 and 7,000 men, was twice as large as the pre-war army and was deployed widely in small garrisons as an internal security force. At first undenominationally Protestant, and a source of official anxiety because many of the soldiers had served in Cromwellian armies, the introduction of obligatory attendance at divine service converted it gradually into a predominantly Anglican force."[25]

James II & VII of Scotland (r. 1685–88)
He was the second son of Charles I and younger brother of Charles II. Following the Civil War, he had been exiled and served in both the French and Spanish Army. Although he converted to Catholicism in 1670, his two daughters were raised as Protestants. Because of his persecution of the Protestant clergy, he was generally hated by the people.

In 1685, following the Monmouth uprising (Monmouth was an illegitimate son of Charles II and a Protestant) and the Bloody Assizes of Judge Jeffries, the Dutch prince, William of Orange who was married to Mary, James II's Protestant daughter, was invited to invade and take the throne.

King James II and Ireland
When James II came to the English throne, fears arose that the landed wealth and political power of Irish Protestants would be greatly undermined. These fears were allayed three years later when James's son-in-law, the Protestant William of Orange, invaded England and claimed the English throne on behalf of his wife, Mary. Needless to say, his actions received strong support among Irish Protestants. James went into exile in France, returning to Ireland in 1689. The subsequent war on Irish soil between William III and James II only served to further exacerbate hostilities between Catholics and Protestants. William III would thereafter be identified as the defender of Irish Protestantism. The year 1690, and the "Battle of the Boyne," still stand out as a defining point in history for Ulster Protestants, because of William's victory over James II and the Irish Catholics who had fought with him. A victory that is celebrated to this day with fervour every 12th July!

William III (r. 1689–1702 and Mary II 1689–94)
William and Mary reigned together until Mary's death in 1694. William then ruled as sole ruler thereafter until his death in 1702. As he grew

up he was educated by various governesses. This was followed by him being taught by a Calvinist teacher, who instructed him regarding Divine Providence and a destiny he was being called to fulfil.

In 1688, a group of politicians invited William to invade England. On the 5th November 1688, he landed in Devon with a fleet of over 450 ships. With local support, his army grew to 20,000 men. They marched on to London in The Glorious Revolution and James II fled to France, where he plotted to regain the throne. As I mentioned above, James landed in Ireland in the following year with French military assistance but was decisively defeated at the Battle of the Boyne and fled again to France, where he died in 1701.

Anne (r. 1702–14)

Anne was the second daughter of James II. It was during Anne's reign (1707) that the United Kingdom of Great Britain was created by the Union of England and Scotland.

That same year an Act for the Relief of the Protestant Purchasers of the forfeited Estates in Ireland was passed. Here is a sample of the general drift of the Acts intent:

> "Sec. 7: *To the end that none of the aforesaid purchased forfeited estates may ever descend to any Papist but shall remain to be held and enjoyed by Protestants for the strengthening of the English interest and Protestant religion,* if any person educated in the popish religion, or professing the same, and being under the age of 18, shall not, within 6 months of attaining the age of 18, take the oath of and supremacy, and the declaration against transubstantiation in the courts of Chancery or Kings-bench in England or Ireland, or in the quarter-sessions where such person shall reside, and continue to be a protestant, such person in respect of himself only, and not his heirs or posterity, shall be disabled to take by decent, devise, or limitation, any of the forfeited estates purchased in Ireland, and during the life of such person, or until he shall take the oaths etc., the protestant next of kin shall enjoy the premises."[26]

Not overly endearing towards Roman Catholics.

***

I now want to look at a series of events which straddled the reign of a number of British monarchs - another pivotal period in Irish history.

Alongside the introduction of the Empire Spirit into Ireland in 1155 and the Reformation, we now have a collection of events: Penal Laws; the United Irishmen; Henry Grattan and the 1782 Constitution; the 1798 Rebellion and the movement toward Emancipation. Flowing out of this we gradually head into the period of the Home Rule Crisis, Civil War and Partition.

Penal Laws

The Penal Laws[27] were a code of laws, starting in 1695 and added to throughout the following 30+ years. They were passed by the Protestant Parliament of Ireland to regulate the status of Roman Catholics through most of the eighteenth century. The ideal was to entice the colonised Irish into wholesale conversion to Anglican Protestantism. They were to curtail the civil, religious, and economic rights of Irish Catholics. It hit Catholic property ownership especially hard. As a result, Catholic land ownership plummeted to negligible levels throughout this period.

Here are a number of the restrictions that the Penal Laws imposed on Irish Catholics:

- No Catholic could have a seat in the Irish Parliament or vote for the election of a Parliamentary candidate.
- A Catholic could not be a judge, a member of the Bar, of the magistracy, or of any municipal corporation.
- A Catholic man was not allowed to serve in the army or navy; he could not be a sheriff, a grand juror, a police constable, or even a parish vestryman.
- He was forbidden to carry any weapon.
- Any Catholic found to have weapons hidden about his person or in his house was liable to be fined, imprisoned, whipped, or put in the pillory, or to undergo a combination of these punishments.
- He could not buy land, inherit it, or even receive it as a gift.

- If the eldest son of a Catholic became a Protestant, he became the owner of whatever estate his father might possess and thus reduced the father to the position of a life tenant.
- A Catholic wife who turned Protestant was legally set free from the control of her husband, and a certain portion of her husband's property or earnings was assigned for her independent use.
- The child of a Catholic had only to profess himself or herself a Protestant in order to be put under the guardianship of some Protestant relative, the father being compelled to pay an annual sum for the bringing up of his offspring.
- So far as the law could accomplish such an end, all manner of education was denied to the Irish Catholic.

Little wonder that issues such as the Penal Laws have left a deep scar in the corporate psyche of Irish Catholicism/Nationalism to this day. Yet, according to the Cambridge History of Ireland, Volume 2, "The penal laws had no effect whatever in suppressing the Catholic religion: we find the Irish parliament in 1723 complaining of the continued increase of Catholicity."[28]

Though not to the same extent, the Penal Laws also affected Presbyterians. They were also denied the vote; their marriages were not recognised by the State and they were required to pay tithes to the Church of Ireland. One of the major effects of the Penal Laws was emigration. Many Irish Catholics and Presbyterians left Ireland looking for a better life elsewhere, often to other areas of Europe, England, Wales, Scotland, or to the Americas.

Yet, even those in political, social and economic dominance in Ireland (The Ascendancy) grappled over their lack of power, as ultimate control still rested with England. Growing out of this would be a reform movement of Irish patriots who began to lobby for representation (albeit for the Protestant middle class only) in parliament. The early seeds of Irish nationalism were being sowed!!

Developments like the War of Independence in America, and the French Revolution, would also have a dominant role to play in spawning the idea of an Irish Republic in the hearts of many Catholics, Presbyterians and a few members of the ascendancy, in which they could be united under a fair and equal governmental system.

In 1782, under Henry Grattan's leadership, an Irish Parliament was established, giving the Irish a limited notion of nationhood - though, still under the Crown. Any ideas of furthering that dream would be shattered by the old rivalries between Catholics and the re-emerging Protestant planters in Ulster. See below: "Henry Grattan (1746-1820)…"

The Society of United Irishmen

As I have already mentioned, Catholics and Presbyterians were collectively exploring the idea of a Republic. In 1791 this resulted in the formation of the United Irishmen "by Theobald Wolfe Tone, James Napper Tandy and Thomas Russell to achieve Roman Catholic emancipation and (with Protestant cooperation) parliamentary reform. British attempts to suppress the society caused its reorganization as an underground movement dedicated to securing complete Irish independence. In April 1794 the society opened negotiations with Revolutionary France for military aid, but the British government soon learned of the activity. Twice in 1796–97 French expeditionary forces failed to reach Ireland. Still anticipating help from France, the United Irishmen made plans for a rebellion in 1798. The principal conspirators were arrested in advance of the uprising, and the meagre aid provided by France came too late to be effective. Only in County Wexford did the rebels make any gains, but they were unable to hold the area, and the rebellion collapsed."[29]

The **Irish Rebellion** in 1798 was an uprising that owed its origins to the Society of United Irishmen. It was established first of all in Belfast and then in Dublin. Its membership was middle-class, with Presbyterians being predominant in the Belfast society, while the Dublin society was made up of Catholics and Protestants. Its main objectives were parliamentary reform, primarily calling for universal male suffrage and complete Catholic emancipation, and the elimination of British rule in Ireland. Even though it failed, under the leadership of Wolfe Tone (regarded as its founding father), the United Irishmen movement can be seen as marking the birth of Republicanism. Tone also became known as the father of the "physical force" tradition – the use of armed struggle.

William Pitt the Younger and Emancipation

The French Revolution revived religious and political problems in

Ireland; a by-product of it was the 1798 rebellion in Ireland. The Prime Minister, William Pitt, firmly believed that the only solution to the problem was the union of Great Britain and Ireland, which was established by the Act of Union in 1800. The following year, Great Britain and Ireland were formally united into a single realm - the United Kingdom of Great Britain and Ireland.[30]

Pitt also sought to inaugurate the new kingdom by granting concessions to the Roman Catholic majority in Ireland, in particular the abolition of various political restrictions under which they suffered. George III, however, did not share the same view. He was strongly opposed to Catholic Emancipation, arguing that to grant additional liberty would violate his coronation oath, in which he had promised to protect the established Church of England. In 1801, Pitt, unable to change the King's strong views, chose to resign.[31]

The birth of the Orange Order

In 1795, the Battle of the Diamond, took place in Co. Armagh, out of which the Orange Order was born.

Background
In July 1795, the Reverend Devine had held a service at Drumcree Church of Ireland Church in Portadown, Co. Armagh, to commemorate the "Battle of the Boyne." The historian Francis Plowden described the events that followed this sermon:

> "Reverend Devine so worked up the minds of his audience, that upon retiring from service, on the different roads leading to their respective homes, they gave full scope to the anti-papistical zeal, with which he had inspired them... falling upon every Catholic they met, beating and bruising them without provocation or distinction, breaking the doors and windows of their houses, and actually murdering two unoffending Catholics in a bog. This unprovoked atrocity of the Protestants revived and redoubled religious rancour. The flame spread and threatened a contest of extermination..."[32]

58

There had been a prevailing atmosphere in Co. Armagh, in which Catholics resented the Protestants and their privileges and the Protestants feared Catholics turning on them. It resulted in a period of intense sectarian fighting throughout the 1780s and 90s between two groups of people: the Ulster Protestant Peep o' Day Boys[33 + Note] and the Roman Catholic Defenders[34 +Note], that culminated in the Battle of the Diamond, during which thirty Defenders were killed.

After the battle, the Peep o' Day Boys met in James Sloan's inn in Loughgall, where they founded the Orange Order[35,36 + Note]. The Reverend Devine was one of the founding members.

Henry Grattan (1746-1820) and the Constitution of 1782

The Irish parliament and its political actions throughout the eighteenth century were solely focused on the Protestant colony in Ireland. In the meantime, the English government continued with its hostile attitude towards Ireland, resulting in ongoing feelings of distrust and aversion in the Irish Parliament and among the colonists.

The struggles of the Irish legislature for independent decision-making, which culminated in Grattan's parliament of 1782, were solely related to the struggles of the Protestants. As a consequence of the Penal Laws, Catholics had no political part to play. He was a major campaigner for reform in the Irish House of Commons and leader of the Patriot Party. [37] The Constitution of 1782 is the series of legal changes which freed the Parliament of Ireland - a parliament established by and subordinate to the Crown of England - of legal restrictions that had been imposed by successive Norman, English, and later, British governments to the scope of its jurisdiction. The most constraining restrictions arose in Poynings' Law of 1495, which had made all legislation passed by the Irish Parliament subject to approval by the British Parliament.

As a member of the ruling Anglo-Irish Protestant class, Grattan became a barrister and in the early 1770s joined the campaign for legislative independence led by Henry Flood. He entered the Irish Parliament in December 1775, soon after Flood had forfeited the movement's leadership by accepting a government office. Grattan's brilliant oratory soon made him the leading spokesman of the parliamentary agitation.

From 1782 to 1797 the movement gained momentum as more and more Irish people came to sympathize with the North American colonists in their war for independence from Great Britain (the American Revolution). By 1779, Grattan was powerful enough to persuade the British government to remove most of its restraints on Irish trade, and in April 1780 he formally demanded the repeal of Poynings' Law.

Two years later, in response to Grattan's demands and to pressure from the Irish Volunteers - a militia organised to defend Ireland against possible French invasion - the British relinquished their right to legislate for Ireland and freed the Irish Parliament from subservience to the English Privy Council.

Grattan continued to make limited progress in his struggle to reform the composition of the Irish Parliament and to win voting rights for Ireland's Roman Catholics. The outbreak of the French Revolution (1789) bolstered his cause by infusing democratic ideas into Ireland, but the subsequent growth of a radical Irish movement for Catholic emancipation provoked repressive measures by the British. Grattan was caught between the two sides. Ill and discouraged, he retired from Parliament in May 1797 and was in England when the Irish radicals staged the unsuccessful Irish Rebellion of 1798.

He returned to Parliament for five months in 1800 and waged a vigorous but fruitless campaign against Prime Minister William Pitt's response to the Rebellion - the Acts of Union (1800). Through them, the Parliament of Ireland was abolished, and the Kingdom of Ireland was absorbed into the new United Kingdom of Great Britain and Ireland, with effect from 1 January 1801.

In 1805 Grattan was elected to the British House of Commons, where for the last 15 years of his life he fought for Catholic emancipation."[38]

In 2005, a newly released six-year study by Dr Danny Mansergh, showed that Grattan mixed with a number of the subversive groups at the time. "He never explicitly advocated violence. He used the implicit threat of force - along the lines of 'if the Government does not act as required, the people will revolt and seize control of the state... His manoeuvring was often very subtle. He had a talent for persuading other people -

the United Irishmen, the Volunteers, the Catholic Committee - to do his public agitating for him."[39]

***

After Anne's death in 1714, the succession should have gone to the nearest Protestant relative of the Stuart line. This would have been Sophia, James I's only daughter, but because she died a few weeks before Anne, the Crown of England was passed by the 1701 Act of Settlement to the Stuart dynasty's German Protestant cousins, the House of Hanover, in the person of King George I, who was fifty-second in line to the throne at that time. That Act effectively excluded the hereditary Stuart heir, James II's Catholic son, James Francis Edward Stuart, from coming to the throne.[40]

Both **George I (r. 1714- 7)** and **George II (r. 1727-60)** exercised little control over British domestic policy, which was largely controlled by Parliament. Coming from a German background they were mostly caught up in European issues.

George III (r. 1760-1820)
George III was perhaps best known for drifting in and out of a state of insanity. Despite that, any idea of emancipation was out of the question. For him, it was not simply a question of pragmatics and politics; it was a religious and personal bottom line, in that the admission of Catholics to public office would run counter to his sacred vow to defend and uphold the Anglican faith. So, to remain true to those coronation vows, he ruled out any possibility of emancipation.

George IV (r. 1821-30)
Opposition to emancipation was set to continue during the reign of George IV. In 1823, Daniel O'Connell commenced a campaign for Catholic emancipation within Great Britain by establishing the Catholic Association. In 1828 he successfully stood in a by-election in Co. Clare, even though he was not allowed to take his seat in the House of Commons of the United Kingdom.

Public opinion was to eventually turn in Britain in favour of emancipation. Politicians understood the critical importance of public opinion. Despite overwhelming support for change, the votes in the House of Lords were

61

consistently negative, in part because of the king's opposition. It took the possibility of a religious civil war in Ireland in 1828-29 to change the balance of opinion in the House of Lords. In 1828 the Sacramental Test Act removed the barrier that required certain public officials to be members of the established Church of England.[41]

William IV (r. 1830-37)
The year before becoming King, as a full supporter of Catholic emancipation, William IV managed, with a few hiccups, to get his brother George to support the Catholic Relief Bill. On the 13th April 1829 it was passed into law, giving Catholics the right to vote, become members of Parliament and to work as civil servants or judges.[42]

Another major accomplishment during his reign was the Slavery Abolition Act of 1833, which abolished slavery in most of the British colonies.

Queen Victoria (r. 1837-1901) and The Great Famine (1845-52)
It was during her reign that the name "Constitutional Monarch" was introduced. The constitutional writer Walter Bagehot identified the monarch as the "dignified part" rather than the "efficient part" of government.

In 2017, the story of Queen Victoria was serialised in a BBC drama called "Victoria." Journalist Frances Mulraney pointed out that it:

> "… drew surprise from British viewers… for the extent to which the Irish suffered both during the 1840s famine and while under English rule, which was finally brought to their attention. While a defining period in Irish history, it is sadly widely uncovered by the British educational system. The role that Britain's Queen Victoria played in coming to the aid of her then-subjects, however, was pushed into the spotlight with the airing of the episodes… British viewers were truly shocked to discover the brutality of the Great Hunger. Many of them had not previously known of the death of at least one million and the emigration of a further million of their closest neighbours in what must be regarded as the darkest and most horrifying seven years in Irish history.

Many commended the episode for finally portraying the devastating horrors of the Irish famine on British TV screens for the first time. Much praise was heaped onto screenwriter Daisy Goodwin for not shying away from the rather unpalatable role the British landlords and government played in the disaster."

Historian Christine Kinealy, founding director of Ireland's Great Hunger Institute at Quinnipiac University, said that, counter to popular thought,

> "There is no evidence that she had any real compassion for the Irish people in any way... We know that she [Queen Victoria] really had no interest in Ireland and so to imagine she wanted to do more doesn't really ring true... In her very long reign, she only visited Ireland four times and one of those times was 1849 when the famine was still raging but coming to an end. At that point, she didn't do anything..."

Not only did Queen Victoria fail to rise to the challenge of protecting the Irish people, the monarchy and those working for it also went out of their way to prevent others from outshining the queen's own mediocre attempts e.g., preventing a significant amount of money from making its way to Ireland from Turkey.

> "She was urged by her Prime Minister Russell to do something for Ireland and so, in January 1847 she issued a Queen's letter asking protestants to raise money for the Irish... In January 1848, she also made her own donation, significantly to a British agency, [of] £2,000. She is the first person named on their records as having given money but because she gave £2,000, it was the Royal protocol that nobody could give more than the monarch... We do have documentation that the Sultan of Turkey, who was himself a very young man at the time, offered to give £10,000 but, in Constantinople, the British embassy went to his people to say that it would offend royal protocol so he reduced his donation [to £1000]."

When she did pay a visit in 1849 it was mainly to the east coast of the country where the worst of the Irish famine was over. Kinealy states:

> "She didn't see it first hand in that sense and we know that there was a very high military presence and that any trouble was suppressed and people were arrested... I don't think at that time people blamed her for the famine to some extent, that interpretation comes a bit later... I think Britain has yet to confront its past... and the famine is definitely an unpalatable aspect of that relationship... English and British people, in general, have very little knowledge of Irish history and that's a real shame because so much of our history is intertwined and that's really something that should be addressed.""[43]

The Irish struggle for independence continues

In *Heal Not Lightly*, I write:

> "During the early 1800's, the liberalising influences of The Enlightenment were instrumental in the voices of Catholics and liberal Protestants being raised regarding Catholic emancipation. This was attained under the leadership of Daniel O'Connell, resulting in the repealing of the Penal Laws in 1829, though the confiscation of the Catholic land during the Penal Law time was to have disastrous consequences in the middle of the nineteenth century, when Ireland was struck with the Great Famine. A population of over eight million people, predominantly poor rural dwellers, was decimated when for two years in a row the potato crop failed. During the first year the government aid was poorly administered and in the following year a new government adopted a policy of non-intervention – starvation, typhus and exposure took their toll: one million people died and a further one million risked the "coffin ships" as they fled to America.

64

Not surprisingly, the famine left its mark deep in the psyche of Irish Catholic people, regarding the British administration. Further attempts at revolution fizzled out and it took the emergence of the Nationalist Party under Parnell, towards the end of that century, to firmly establish constitutional nationalism in Ireland. This was to produce a strong reaction from many Ulster Protestants. When the British Government made several attempts at introducing the Home Rule Bill, the stage was being set for stiff resistance by "whatever means necessary" to be formalised in The Ulster Covenant of 1912."[44]

The Home Rule era

Without going into too much detail, Wikipedia gives a broad overview of the period.

"The Irish Home Rule movement was a movement that campaigned for self-government (or "home rule') for Ireland within the United Kingdom of Great Britain and Ireland. It was the dominant political movement of Irish nationalism from 1870 to the end of World War I.

Isaac Butt founded the Home Government Association in 1870. This was succeeded in 1873 by the Home Rule League, and in 1882 by the Irish Parliamentary Party. These organisations campaigned for home rule in the British House of Commons. Under the leadership of Charles Stewart Parnell, the movement came close to success when the Liberal government of William Ewart Gladstone introduced the first Home Rule Bill in 1886, but the bill was defeated in the House of Commons after a split in the Liberal Party. After Parnell's death, Gladstone introduced the Second Home Rule Bill in 1893; it passed the Commons but was defeated in the House of Lords. After the removal of the Lord's veto in 1911, the Third Home Rule Bill was introduced in 1912, leading to the Home Rule Crisis. Shortly after the outbreak of World War I it was enacted, but implementation was suspended until the conclusion of the war."[45]

It was during this time, 1912-1916, that the issues surrounding the Ulster Covenant and the Easter Rising took place.

The Ulster Covenant (1912)

I will now include here extracts from my book "Heal Not Lightly."

> "In 1886 when the British Liberal Party first introduced the first Home Rule Bill. It provoked a very hostile reaction from many shades of Irish Protestantism. Following special meetings of the Church of Ireland Synod, the Presbyterian Church's General Assembly and the Methodist Conference all parties produced resolutions, strongly critical of the Bill. The Methodist Church in its denominational paper wrote: "Home Rule for Ireland means not only war against the crown rights of England, but against the crown rights of Christ… its inspiration is religious antipathy, its methods plunder, its object Protestant annihilation." (Pg. 22).

And then from Pages 23-26: Regarding the third introduction of Bill in 1912, R. Finlay G. Holmes, former Professor of Church History at the Presbyterian Church's Union Theological College, Belfast, writes:

> "[So] the crisis did not come upon the Unionists "As a thief in the night" … from the beginning, their defiance was articulated and encouraged by leading prominent churchmen. On the eve of the general election of 1910 which brought the Liberals to power, eleven former moderators of the Irish Presbyterian Assembly took the unprecedented step of publishing a manifesto in which they contended that the best interests of all the people of Ireland were safeguarded by the union with Great Britain… an independent Irish parliament, however would reverse this process and establish a Roman

Catholic ascendancy with "clerical control" even in matters that were "purely civil and secular."[46] (Pg.23).

Protestation to the contrary by men like John Dillon that "they would no more take their political guidance from the pope of Rome... or conduct their affairs at the bidding of any body of cardinals", if they had even been heard, were not believed. The Moderator of the General Assembly of 1912, Henry Montgomery, an earnest evangelical... declared that "such promises and pledges are not worth the breath used in speaking them or the ink required to write them."

On February 1st 1912 a convention of Irish Presbyterians was held in the Assembly Hall in Belfast, with overflow meetings in some inner-city churches... it attracted considerable support from Presbyterians in general, and the Witness (the Presbyterian Newspaper - *mine*) rejoiced in its unequivocal reaffirmation of the opposition to Home Rule previously expressed in 1886 and 1893. Some of the speakers who addressed the convention did not shrink from the ultimate implications of their position. T.G. Houston, Head Master of a leading Grammar School, insisted that no sacrifice was too great for their noble cause: "In the last resort they should be prepared to sacrifice even life itself rather than yield to what would prove the ruin of themselves and their country." He warned the government that their threats were not "empty vapour." They were made, not in jingo, but in a martyr spirit.

This Presbyterian convention received a message of support from the Church of Ireland Primate, Archbishop Crozier, assuring them that their action "in the present terrible crisis" would be followed by a similar demonstration of Anglican feeling. The vice-president of the Irish Baptist Union offered the convention his "heart-sympathy" and shortly afterwards Irish Methodists held a similar assembly to express opposition to home rule.

Undoubtedly many elements combined to make Ulster Protestants' resistance to Home Rule the implacable force it became - religious conviction and prejudice, economic self-interest, national consciousness and culture, perhaps even, as Joseph Lee has suggested, racialism. "Racialism, articulated in religious idiom, dominated Scotch-Irish hostility to Home Rule." The economic arguments of the Unionists, he believes, had racialist overtones, successful Ulster businessmen suspecting that the Celt was incapable of mastering the industrial virtues.

In 1912 Ulster Unionists, with the blessing of Protestant church leaders, were preparing to fight in the original words of Randolph Churchill "Ulster will fight and Ulster will be right." On Easter Tuesday in 1912, 100,000 men paraded at Balmoral... in an impressive show of strength which began with a religious service led by the Church of Ireland primate and the Moderator of the General Assembly.

The Witness continued to pour out scorn on those who did not share the majority view that resistance to Home Rule, even in arms, was a sacred duty.

An editorial in July 1912 read:

> "There are some who say that this is an unwise and unchristian attitude, that the prudent and Christian attitude should be for the Ulster Protestants to lick the rod and bite the dust and lie down and let the conquerors trample over them; better chains of slavery than resistance... it is a peace at the price of freedom... a peace at too great a price. For weal or woe it will not be paid."

The Witness Dublin correspondent wrote:

> "How can it be affirmed that we are transgressing the law of Christ? The New Testament does not teach nations the law of non-resistance any more than the Old. In 1690 our forefathers... successfully fought our great battle for civil and religious liberty. What sort of spurious Christianity is this that tells us that we must not lift up a voice in protest or a hand in defence? God's witnesses in all generations cry shame on such a proposition."

F.E. Smith was quoted as asking an assembly of Orangemen on the 12th July: "If we are not prepared to die for our faith, in the name of God and of men what is there we would die for?"

The dread implications of Home Rule were reiterated ad nauseam... The determination of Orangemen to resist was undiminished, "Unless the Cabinet drops its mad policy there can be no escape except in a baptism of blood."

The climax and supreme demonstration of the Ulster Protestants' determination was the signing of the Ulster Covenant on 28th September, 1912, known as Ulster Day. The text of the Covenant was largely the work of the Presbyterian ruling elder, Thomas Sinclair, and recalled the historic Scottish covenants, which occupied a hallowed place in Presbyterian memories and imaginations. It was, Joseph Lee has suggested, "the traditional technique of reminding God whose side He was on." It pledged its signatories, "humbly relying on the God whom our fathers trusted... to stand by one another in defending for ourselves and our children our cherished position of equal citizenship in the United Kingdom, and in using all means which may be found necessary to defeat the present conspiracy to set up a home rule parliament in Ireland." 237,368 men signed it and 234,046 women signed a parallel Declaration at over 300 centres throughout Ireland."[47]

It is my understanding that the many sermons and political speeches made throughout this period stirred up a hatred and fear of the Roman Catholic Church (a selection of which can be read in the first chapter of my book). They were being used to unite Protestantism in an act of rebellion, against the Government in Westminster. I believe this was a misuse of God's name and scripture. I can't help but wonder what might have happened if the Churches had been called to prayer and fasting!

Ancient Celtic Mythology and The Easter Rising

In *"Ireland: Blood Sacrifice"* David Blake and Paddy Monaghan, write:

"Before Christianity came to Ireland in the 5th century, our pagan ancestors used to worship many gods, one of whom was the earth goddess called 'Eire', who was regarded as the bride of the king who 'married' her at Tara at his inauguration. From the earliest times Ireland was thought of as a woman and this image continues vividly and powerfully to the present day. Some early writings on this period record that though Eire, symbolising the land, was old and ugly, when a human sacrifice was made to her, she became young and beautiful, a fit bride for the king. Thus, a young man had to be sacrificed, his blood seeping down into the earth. Even before the coming of St. Patrick this practice of human sacrifice was abolished and an animal substituted for the young man. Nevertheless, the memory of the ancient myth, the withered old hag who personified the land being transformed into a beautiful young girl by the blood sacrifice of young men, remained. It has survived in the two images of Ireland with which we are still familiar, the young girl queen Caithlin Ni hUllachain or Roisin Dubh and the old woman, the Sean Bhean Bhoct, the Hag of Beara."

"Every country has its founding fathers and its foundation myth... For the Republic of Ireland, it is the Easter Rising. [In Easter 1916] a small group of revolutionaries took over the centre of Dublin city and held it for a week until it was reduced to rubble by the artillery of the British Army. The leaders, all signatories to the Proclamation of the Irish Republic, were executed. This event, solemnly commemorated every Easter, has become the foundation story of the Irish Republic. It differs in one regard from most other foundation stories. It is a religious as well as a political event. According to Padraig Pearse, Commandant-General of the rebels, they were laying down their lives for Ireland as Christ laid down his life for the world; they were redeeming Ireland with their blood. And they succeeded. A whole new generation of revolutionaries sprang up after them as Pearse... had predicted."[48]

Following the Easter Rising, public support in particular shifted from the Home Rule movement to the more radical Sinn Féin party. In the 1918 General Election the Irish Parliamentary Party suffered a crushing defeat with only a handful of MPs surviving, effectively dealing a death blow to the Home Rule movement. The elected Sinn Féin MPs were not content merely with Home Rule within the framework of the United Kingdom; they instead set up a revolutionary legislature, Dail Éireann, and declared Ireland an independent republic.

Britain passed a Fourth Home Rule Bill, the Government of Ireland Act 1920, aimed at creating separate parliaments for Northern Ireland and Southern Ireland. The former was established in 1921, and the territory continues to this day as part of the United Kingdom, but the latter never functioned. Following the Anglo-Irish Treaty that ended the Anglo-Irish War, twenty-six of Ireland's counties became, in December 1922, the Irish Free State, a dominion within the British Empire. When the Republic of Ireland Act of 1948 came into force in April 1949, Ireland's status as a British dominion ended, and with it its membership in the British Commonwealth of Nations. The rebirthing of Sinn Féin and the IRA in the mid-1960s coincided with the fiftieth anniversary of 1916.[49]

The impasse, as illustrated in the image of the two magnets in the Introduction, continues to be played out in our politics. The issues surrounding Brexit and the Protocol are, I believe, a further manifestation of that.

Part IV

Back to the tree!

I would love to see a discussion developing in which we, as Christians, look at our cultures, without our cultural blindfolds on, realising that all of the events of our juxtapositioned histories are but branches within the same, greater tree and its roots? This is not an issue of taking sides regarding our Catholic and Protestant histories. Rather it should be an objective revisiting. There is much in our histories on this island that we collectively need to understand, own, repent of and be reconciled over, especially in the light of the fact that we have been divided over the same root issue – the spirit of empire! The legacy of colonialism straddles the Reformation.

Both of the juxtapositioned communities here in Northern Ireland actually share the same root. This should be uniting us against a common enemy - Satan!

The issue of the two Covenants (1912 and 1916) is one that is close to my heart. It is a fruit of the root I have brought before you in this book. Given what we are faced with in Northern Ireland – politically, socially and spiritually - it is a fruit that especially needs to be revisited and addressed. In 2 Corinthians 5:19, the Apostle Paul writes that God *"has committed to us the message of reconciliation."* Regarding this, I believe that we, the Church in this land, are being called by God to live out this message. I feel especially for the Protestant clergy - and I have talked to many over the years - who have told me that they had been 'banging their heads against a wall' throughout their ministry, against Orangeism, Freemasonry and the altars of Protestant Nationalism. As Clergy, they need to take the lead, and yet I am aware that their hands are tied by so much that is sectarian within their denominations and their congregations. They need our prayers.

How Irish Nationalism can address the Covenant of 1916, is not immediately clear to me. It was not initiated by the Catholic Church, yet its presence in Ireland over many centuries has meant that it is profoundly intertwined in the political and spiritual life of this island, including 1916. It would be good to see a reciprocal response from within Irish Nationalism. Perhaps after the Protestant and Catholic Churches have acknowledged and repented regarding their roles, such a response might be forthcoming! Demographic changes in Northern Ireland would suggest that at some point a referendum on the North-South border will produce a result in favour of a United Ireland. Even with the Election results in May 2022 which gave Sinn Féin the majority of seats in the Assembly, opinion Polls tell us that a Referendum regarding the Border is still some time off. Nevertheless, how should the Governing bodies of the churches in the thirty-two counties be preparing for that? A new narrative needs to be articulated!

Anything that feeds into our national/cultural identity that has non-Christian spiritual roots: Irish Nationalism or Northern Irish Protestant Nationalism – if we invoke these to validate our cultural or political stance, we are invoking the spirit of nationalism. This is idolatry!

We are a Kingdom of God people...

Throughout my writing of this booklet, I have constantly had in my mind that as Christians we are first of all a Kingdom of God people. Sadly, as you have read, we have all too often, mistakenly been serving another kingdom through embracing the 'empire spirit.'

When we think of the word 'kingdom,' we think of a region or a territory that is ruled by a king or a queen, e.g., the United Kingdom of Great Britain and Northern Ireland. But when we think of the Kingdom of God, Jesus spoke of it as something that is not limited to a specific area of land. It is rather "the dynamic reign of God over heaven and earth, visible and invisible."[50] As God is eternal, so is His Kingdom. Likewise, like Him, it transcends time and space.

In Matthew 6:33, Jesus told us to *"But seek first his kingdom and his righteousness..."* When he stood before Pilate he said, *"My kingdom is not of this world."* (John 18:36) and in Psalm 103:19, we read: *"The Lord*

73

has established his throne in heaven, and his kingdom rules over all."
Also, in Luke 17:21 we read that the kingdom of God resides within us.
So, when Jesus taught that the kingdom is within the believer, he was
pointing out to us the new spiritual realm in which we are now supposed
to live – it is individual and yet collective; redemptive and restorative –
borne out by his quote from Isaiah 61:1:

> *"The Spirit of the Sovereign Lord is on me, because
> the Lord has anointed me to proclaim good news to
> the poor. He has sent me to bind up the brokenhearted,
> to proclaim freedom for the captives and release from
> darkness for the prisoners."*

The kingdom of God cannot be established by non-kingdom means.
All of this is a particular challenge for Christians who hold leadership
positions in the community as a politician or Church leader, they are
meant to serve it as a Kingdom of God citizen. If we embrace the ways
of the kingdom of this world in that ministry, then we are no longer
serving the purposes of God!

The expansion of the Kingdom of God in Ireland is so counter to this and
it has been hampered by continuing to allow/enable our congregations
to embrace it. The Spirit of God has been quenched, grieved. It is
estimated that at least 85% of Protestant men signed the Ulster Covenant
in 1912. That means that many young men in our congregations are
the 4th generation, from their grandfathers who signed it. What are the
implications of that for the historic denominational churches, trans
denominations ministries and all the new churches springing up all over
Ireland?

In light of what I have laid down in this booklet, issues relating to the
Ulster Covenant need to be revisited. Well established principles of
engagement against "the principalities and powers" have shown that
if a governing body of a Church leads its people into sin, thus giving
Satan a foothold within it, then that governing body (or its generational
descendants) needs to repent of it, hence breaking that foothold!
(Nehemiah 1:6, Ephesians 4:26-27). Meanwhile, individual followers of
Christ can, through repentance, remove the influence of this generational
foothold of Satan in their lives.

It is worth mentioning here that while Ireland is now divided into two different political entities it is still one spiritually. The governing bodies of all our main churches represent the 32 counties of Ireland. Any decisions they make, such as underscoring the Ulster Covenant, affect the whole island! Something I feel the Churches in the Republic of Ireland need to be mindful of.

I would love to see a movement within the Governing bodies of the Presbyterian, Church of Ireland and Methodist Churches, to look afresh at this, with a view of repenting of their role in endorsing the Ulster Covenant. Not with any sectarian, political agendas but solely for *"the Kingdom of God and His righteousness."* To seek His face, embrace His heart!

I would love to see a movement of prayer rising up to come against the *"principalities and powers"* operating in this land. The "return of the glory," as John Dawson put it, needs to be born out of humbling ourselves, seeking God's face and repenting of our "wicked ways." (See 2 Chronicles 7:14)

Many unanswered questions still remain

Approximately 18 years ago, two church leaders encouraged me to write *"Heal Not Lightly"* - a former Church of Ireland Bishop and a former Presbyterian Moderator. Back then, one of them told me that he would bring it into the governing body of his church if he thought he had a quorum – which he felt he didn't. The other one more recently told me that he was rereading the book and made the comment, "There's a lot of unfinished business in it!"

As mentioned above, retired Clergy have told me that throughout their entire ministry, they have struggled because of the influence of Orangeism and Freemasonry in their church leaders and congregations! Another told me that he had read my book and that he agreed with what I had written but could not speak about the issue from his pulpit as it would have divided his congregation and jeopardised his ministry.

There is a lot of unfinished business here! There is also a real issue of fear here! We need to understand more fully what Paul meant when he wrote in Ephesians 6:12, *"For our struggle is not against flesh and blood, but against the rulers, against the authorities, against the powers of this dark world and against the spiritual forces of evil in the heavenly realms."* He is telling us that our centuries-old struggle is not against flesh and blood – "us" against "them"! The bottom line is this, Satan is seeking to thwart God's purposes, the Kingdom of God for Ireland!!

The challenge – how do we address this in our churches? How do we go forward? What about that quorum? It has been suggested to me that instead of looking to the top levels of leadership to embrace it, there may be mileage in seeking to build one from the bottom up. What would small informal gatherings of like-minded Clergy and congregants from within a particular denomination, around a coffee, look like – during which they would be willing to look at some of the discussion points raised at the end of this booklet? What would happen in the training of ministers, if they had sessions included in their curriculum, that address the issues raised by the Doctrine of Discovery and its impact on Ireland's political and spiritual roots and the misuse of covenant?

We say we want healing in the land. We say we want revival. We say we want a new outpouring of the Holy Spirit. We pray 2 Chronicles 7:14 but we seem to get stuck at *"humble themselves"*! And what exactly are *"our wicked ways"*? What does that mean for us as Christians – Catholic/Protestant, Nationalist/Unionist Christians – here in Ireland?

As we meet in our churches to pray for our communities, our country, how can we, with integrity, do this if we are not facing these issues? How can God answer our prayers when we have not let go of our sectarian attitudes? How can God answer, when we have not removed the "high places" in the land, the altars to our gods of Ulster Protestant/Irish Catholic Nationalism?

Can we lay down the idolatry of our nationalisms? Can we embrace what it means to be a "Kingdom of God" people? As you finish reading this booklet, is God asking anything of you?

Can we see in the bigger picture, the work of Satan in our Island – especially where it was/is taking place both in and through the Church?

Can we objectively look at our own history and the history of the other? Will we allow the Holy Spirit to do this in us?

The prophetic role of the Church is to repent for what we have wrongly done in the land and give a courageous lead. God is calling us to the ministry of reconciliation, to be His healers in the land.

If colonialism was wrong in America regarding genocide and the theft of Native American land, then surely it cannot be right here? The stark reality is that I, as a descendant of the Planters, am also living on stolen land! There is healing in acknowledgement!

Equally, how many Irish Catholic Nationalists are genetically offspring of colonialism under the Normans and Old English who were as equally persecuted by the British Crown – before and after the Reformation? More English than they thought!

Part V

Conculsion

To finish, I'm back to my book, *"Heal Not Lightly."* and the image of the beaver dam. Back to the River of God.

Ezekiel. 47:1-12. *"When I arrived there, I saw a great number of trees on each side of the river. He said to me, "This water flows toward the eastern region and goes down into the Arabah, where it enters the Dead Sea. When it empties into the sea, the salty water there becomes fresh. Swarms of living creatures will live wherever the river flows. There will be large numbers of fish, because this water flows there and makes the salt water fresh; so,* **where the river flows everything will live**... *Fruit trees of all kinds will grow on both banks of the river. Their leaves will not wither, nor will their fruit fail. Every month they will bear fruit, because the water from the sanctuary flows to them. Their* **fruit** *will serve for food and their leaves for* **healing.***""*

John 7:37-39. *"On the last and greatest day of the festival, Jesus stood and said in a loud voice, "Let anyone who is thirsty come to me and drink. Whoever believes in me, as Scripture has said, rivers of living water will flow from within them." By this he meant the Spirit, whom those who believed in him were later to receive..."*

We, the Church, are now that temple. The river of God should be flowing out of us, flooding this land. Sadly, our divided painful history led to the drawing up of the two Covenants - we continue to live out of the consequences, both spiritually and politically. Through endorsing the Ulster Covenant the major Protestant denominational Churches, more or less, blocked the flow of that river. It has been my prayer, the longing of my heart to see that river flowing in its fullness again, bringing life, fruitfulness and healing!

In this booklet, I have sought to sow seeds, hopefully into many lives. What I have laid out in it, will in all likelihood, not bring significant changes overnight, but my fervent hope and prayer is that in time, seeds will germinate, and understanding will lead to repentance and ultimate change.

A few years back someone shared with me an image God had given them of a "good root system." Interestingly it was regarding Celtic Christianity. The tree had been cut down, but its deep root system remained intact. As I have already mentioned, there is a lot of renewed interest in Celtic Spirituality today – a looking back to the pre-Catholic Christianity, which developed and sustained itself out on the western edges of Europe. While we can over-romanticise "Celtic Christianity," they nevertheless preserved the scriptures, lived in dynamic communities and had a rhythm of prayer and worship which in places like Bangor Abbey were active for centuries. The Celtic Church was also largely Messianic in nature, keeping Sabbath and the Feasts. The seeds from it, spread throughout Europe, as they pioneered the gospel. Good seed and roots - can a new expression of its DNA grow again?

"Everyone loves the idea of reconciliation... until it involves truth-telling, confessing, repenting, dismantling, forgiving, and peace-making." Eugene Cho.

"May your Kingdom come, may your will be done in Ireland, as it is in heaven."

Do it Lord, in and through me.

Points to Ponder...

A selection of questions which may be useful for individual consideration and/or small group discussion:

1. This book reveals something of Harry's journey in reconciliation. What is yours?

2. When Henry II furthered the demise of the Celtic Church in Ireland in the 12th century, he introduced Christendom, not Christianity. What is the difference and which model is the Church in Ireland embracing today?

3. As Christians, we are all on a journey into wholeness in Christ. How should this apply to our cultural identity?

4. What informs your worldview? How much of it is true to or counter to a Christian worldview?

5. What defines a Catholic Irish Nationalist or an Ulster Protestant Unionist Nationalist culture? How do these differ from a Kingdom of God Culture?

6. How can we in the Church, individually and collectively, redeem the past wrongs in our histories?

7. What are the implications of the Doctrine of Discovery for the Church regarding discipleship and evangelism today?

8. If "Our battle is not against flesh and blood (us v them)," why do we fight one another within the body of Christ?

9. What are the implications of the Doctrine of Discovery before and after the Reformation, for the Church and Politics in the Ireland of tomorrow?

10. What most challenged you as you read this book?

11. What can you take from this booklet that will inform your next steps? What should your next steps be?

References

1. Harry Smith, *"Heal Not Lightly."* New Wine Ministries. Pub. 2006.
2. Harry Smith, *"A Destiny Denied... A Dignity Restored."* World Wide Publishing Group. Pub. 2019.
3. Dallas Willard. *"The Spirit of the Disciplines: Understanding how God changes lives."* HarperSanFrancisco. Reprint, Pub. 2002.
4. John Dawson, *"Taking your Cities for God."* Charisma House, Copyright 2001. Pg. 53-54.
5. John Dawson, *"What Christians Should Know About Reconciliation."* Sovereign World Ltd. Pub. 1998. Pgs. 12-13.
6. Alden T. Vaughan, *"New England Frontier, Puritans and Indians, 16220-1675."* 3rd Edition, University of Oklahoma Press, Pub. 1995. Pg. 145.
7. https://en.wikipedia.org/wiki/Papal_bull
8. Harry Smith, *"A Destiny Denied... A Dignity Restored."* Pg. 29. World Wide Publishing Group. Pub. 2019.
9. Robert Williams, *"The American Indian in Western Legal Thought: The Discourse of Conquest."* Oxford University Press. Pub. 1990. Pg. 29.
10. Robert Miller in *"Native America Discovered and Conquered-Thomas Jefferson, Lewis and Clarke and Manifest Destiny,"* University of Nebraska Press. Pub. 2008. Pg. 13.
11. Anthony Pagden's, "Lords of all the World: Ideologies of Empire in Spain, Britain and France c.1500-c.1800," Yale University Press, revised edition. 1998.
12. Robert Miller in *"Native America Discovered and Conquered-Thomas Jefferson, Lewis and Clarke and Manifest Destiny,"* University of Nebraska Press. Pub. 2008. Pg. 15.
13. www.expaedia.org/wiki/Hiberno-Roman_relations
14. Pelagianism – from the British monk Pelagius, who prompted a school of thought that denied several fundamental Christian doctrines e.g., original sin, the fall of man, and salvation by grace. https://www.learnreligions.com/what-is-pelagianism-4783772

15. St. Palladius. https://www.newadvent.org/cathen/11424a.htm https://en.m.wikipedia.org/wiki/Palladius_(bishop_of_Ireland)
16. St. Patrick. Sources: https://www.irishcatholic.com/christians-in-ireland-before-patrick/ and Atlas of Irish History, Sean Duffy, Gill & McMillan, Pgs. 16, 20, 22.)
17. The *Laudibiliter.* https://www.libraryireland.com/HullHistory/Appendix1a.php
18. https://www.historyextra.com/period/medieval/king-john-evil-ireland-monster-nicholas-vincent-magna-carta/
19. https://en.wikipedia.org/wiki/Henry_III_of_England
20. From an article by Dr John Scally, professor in ecclesiastical history at Trinity College Dublin. https://www.irishtimes.com/opinion/why-did-the-reformation-fail-to-take-hold-in-an-ireland-under-english-rule-1.3249598
21. https://en.wikipedia.org/wiki/Plantation_of_Ulster
22. Neil Hegarty, *"The Story of Ireland."* BBC Books. Pub. 2011. Pgs.123-124.
23. Ohlmeyer & Kentyon, The Civil Wars, A Military History of England, Scotland and Ireland, 1638-60, pg.74. Oxford University Press; First Edition 1998.
24. Padraig Lenihan, Confederate Catholics at War, Cork University Press, 2001. pg. 31.
25. https://www.encyclopedia.com/international/encyclopedias-almanacs-transcripts-and-maps/restoration-ireland
26. https://www.law.umn.edu/library/irishlaw/chron-anne
27. Penal Laws. https://www.libraryireland.com/irelandherstory/the-penal-laws.php and http://www.aughty.org/pdf/penallaws.pdf
28. Source: The Cambridge History of Ireland Vol. 2. Jane Ohlmeyer and Thomas Bartlett. Pg 309.
29. https://www.britannica.com/topic/Society-of-United-Irishmen
30. https://www.britannica.com/event/Irish-Rebellion-Irish-history-1798 and https://en.wikipedia.org/wiki/Irish_Rebellion_of_1798
31. https://www.newworldencyclopedia.org/entry/William_Pitt_the_Younger
32. Francis Plowden. *"History of Ireland Vol I-3."* British Lib. Pub.
33. https://en.wikipedia.org/wiki/Armagh_disturbances
Note: The name Peep o' Day Boys came from the early morning

raiding of Catholic homes. The reason for these raids initially seems to have been to confiscate illegally held weapons, but this may well have been merely a pretext for the raids. The reality was that Protestant feared an end to their domination over Catholics if they gained equal access to weapons. The raids soon not only focused on confiscating arms, but also on looting, hooliganism, smashing and destroying weaving equipment as well as the raiding and wrecking of homes.

34. https://en.wikipedia.org/wiki/Defenders_(Ireland)
   Note: The Defenders were a Roman Catholic agrarian secret society founded in County Armagh in the mid-1780s. Initially, they were formed as local defensive organisations opposed to the Protestant Peep o' Day Boys. However, by 1790, they had become a secret oath-bound fraternal society made up of lodges. By 1796, the Defenders had allied with the United Irishmen and participated in the 1798 Rebellion.

35. https://www.bbc.co.uk/news/uk-northern-ireland-18769781
   Note: The Orange Order is a 'fraternal' organisation, named after William of Orange (King William III), the Protestant Dutchman who seized the throne of Catholic King James II back in the 'Glorious Revolution' of 1688. Two years later, 'King Billy' defeated James at the Battle of the Boyne near Drogheda, Co. Louth. He is revered by the Orange Order as a champion of their faith and the man who secured the Protestant ascendancy in Ireland. It also strengthened resistance in Ulster to the Home Rule Bill of 1912 and has continued as a bastion of Protestant Unionist opinion. It also has links to what is known as Ulster Loyalism.[36 + Note Below]

36. https://en.wikipedia.org/wiki/Ulster_loyalism
   Note: Ulster Loyalism "is a strand of Ulster Unionism associated predominantly with working class Ulster Protestants... Like most unionists, they are loyal to the British monarchy, support the continued existence of Northern Ireland within the United Kingdom, and oppose a united Ireland... Loyalism began as a self-determination movement of Ulster Protestants who did not want to become part of an autonomous Ireland... Historically, the terms 'unionist' and 'loyalist' were often interchangeable, but since the beginning of the 'troubles,' 'loyalist' is often used when referring to paramilitary unionism. Loyalists are also said to be loyal primarily to the Protestant British monarchy rather than to British governments

and institutions."

37. https://www.libraryireland.com/JoyceHistory/George.php
38. https://www.britannica.com/biography/Henry-Grattan and https://en.wikipedia.org/wiki/Constitution_of_1782
39. https://www.independent.ie/entertainment/books/grattans-aid-to-1798-men-of-violence-26208238.html
40. https://www.englishmonarchs.co.uk/hanover_11.html
41. https://en.wikipedia.org/wiki/Catholic_emancipation
42. https://www.totallytimelines.com/king-william-iv-of-great-britain-and-ireland-1765-1837/
43. Originally published in February 2018. https://www.irishcentral.com/roots/history/queen-victoria-irish-famine
44. Harry Smith, *"Heal Not Lightly."* New Wine Ministries. Pub. 2006. Pgs. 57-58.
45. https://en.wikipedia.org/wiki/Irish_Home_Rule_movement
46. Source: Studies in Church History, Vol. 20, The Church and War.
47. Source: *"Heal Not Lightly."* Pgs. 22-27.
48. Source: *"Ireland: The Blood Sacrifice."* David Blake and Paddy Monaghan.
49. https://en.m.wikipedia.org/wiki/Irish_Home_Rule_movement
50. Source: *"What is The Kingdom of God?"* A Vineyard Churches UK & Ireland publication. Pg. 7.

My books.

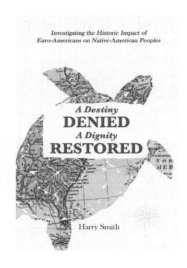

Heal Not Lightly.
This book is currently only available from me and can be bought for £7.00stg (€9.00) including postage. Email me at harry@dignityrestored.org to give me your postal address. Payable through: paypal.me/dignityrestored or Cheque: payable to W H Smith.

A Destiny Denied... A Dignity Restored.
U.K.: http://bit.ly/destinybook-UK
Also available as an ebook on Amazon.

- Dignity Restored -
Email: harry@dignityrestored.org
Web: www.dignityrestored.org